I wish to express my love and gratitude to my partner Mike, a professional chef, for his culinary expertise and advice; to Kathryn Hill, my guardian angel, co-administrator and social media manager; to Jason Friedman, my co-administrator and photographer extraordinaire; to The Gentle Chef group moderators on Facebook: Theresa (aka Sasse), Birgit and Malinda; and to all of our wonderful Facebook group members for their continuing support and encouragement.

This book is dedicated to you…

On the cover: A cascade of Golden Cheese Sauce crowning a steamed broccoli floret. Photograph courtesy of Jason Friedman.

Email: thegentlechef@gmail.com

Website: http://thegentlechef.com

ISBN-13: 978-1484811221

Table of Contents

Non-Dairy Treats   135

For questions and advice regarding the recipes,
please join the Gentle Chef Group on Facebook:
https://www.facebook.com/groups/thegentlechef

To view the full-color photo gallery of the recipes in this book,
please visit The Gentle Chef website at: http://thegentlechef.com

Introduction

While abstaining from meat comes easy to some, abstaining from dairy foods remains the greatest obstacle for many who consider or attempt the transition to a plant-based diet. For many established vegans, commercial non-dairy foods are often not satisfying, whether due to lack of flavor or inaccurate flavor, odd texture, the inclusion of too many refined and processed ingredients or simply lack of availability.

The Non-Dairy Formulary is a continuation, and in many cases, a revision of my work with non-dairy and egg-free recipes from my first publication, The Gentle Chef Cookbook. In this new book, I've incorporated many different and new ingredients and techniques to create non-dairy foods that are as similar to their dairy counterparts as possible. If some recipes appear repeated it's because the ingredients and/or techniques have been modified or improved in some way or are essential to the other recipes.

Hopefully with so many tasty new options, cravings will be satisfied and there will be no more excuses for continuing dairy and egg consumption. I think you'll be delighted with the flavors and textures that these new recipes provide; however, please keep in mind that my formulations are based upon distant memories of dairy flavors and textures. It's been many years since I've consumed dairy and egg products, so if you've recently transitioned to non-dairy foods and have a keen memory, my interpretations may not match your interpretations exactly.

Cooking is an art, but producing non-dairy foods is a science, much like the science of baking. The recipes depend upon accurate measurements and "eye-balling" measurements or making substitutions can result in poor or failed results. When and if substitutions can be made, they will be indicated.

You won't find a great deal of nutrition information included with the recipes. That's not what this book is about. The primary goal of this book is to break the reliance on animal-based foods for ethical reasons and secondly, to provide superior alternatives to commercial non-dairy foods. Non-dairy creams, cheeses and desserts are not intended to be staples of the plant-based diet. Some of the recipes contain significant amounts of plant fat and calories. These foods are intended to be consumed in moderation as a pleasurable and satisfying addition to a well-balanced plant-based diet. The recipes were created using wholesome ingredients as much as possible and refined ingredients were included only when absolutely necessary to achieve proper textures.

My recipes are not the only way to produce these foods, nor are they necessarily the best way. They're simply my way based upon what has worked for me. Creating high quality non-dairy foods is a complex art and there is no doubt that I have many discoveries to make in the future. The recipes will continue to evolve as I continue to learn. I invite you to join me on my journey of discovery... Skye, The Gentle Chef

The Non-Dairy Pantry

Some of the ingredients and kitchen tools in this book may be very familiar and others may not be familiar at all. Before attempting the recipes, it's helpful to familiarize yourself with these items and understand what they are and why they are being used.

Agar powder is a tasteless seaweed derivative and a widely used vegan replacement for gelatin. It is used, when appropriate, as a firming and gelling agent and is especially useful for creating custard-like textures in desserts.

Agar is not heat-reversible, in other words, once set it will not re-melt, at least not completely. Therefore it is not the best option for preparing cheeses when smooth melting is a desired characteristic; nor is it the best option when a very strong gelling agent is required, such as for the soymilk-based block cheeses in this book.

Agar is also available in flake form (and occasionally stick form), but the powdered form dissolves more readily in hot liquid and ounce per ounce is more economical (at least this has been my experience). For this reason, I now only use and recommend the powdered form. Agar powder can be purchased in most health food and natural food stores or online through food retail websites such as Amazon.com.

Ancho chili powder is made from dried, ground poblano chili peppers and has a low Scoville value relative to other powdered chilies (the Scoville value is the measurement of the pungency, or spicy heat, of chili peppers). The rich, sweet flavor of ancho is popular among many chili cooks and commonly found in tamales and mole sauces. Ancho chili powder is specified when a red pepper flavor is desired without over-powering heat. If you cannot find ancho chili powder specifically, most stores carry standard "chili powder" in their spice sections, and these powders are usually very mild.

Arrowroot powder is a starch obtained from the rhizomes (rootstock) of several tropical plants, traditionally *Maranta arundinacea*, but also from Florida arrowroot (*Zamia pumila*). It is a food thickening agent and can be used in equal amounts as a substitute for unmodified potato starch and cornstarch.

Carrageenan is a seaweed derivative that has been used in cooking for hundreds of years as a thickening, stabilizing and gelling agent. Carrageenan is produced in three forms, Iota, Kappa and Lambda, and is widely used in many commercial vegan foods, such as salad dressings, veggie dogs, plant milks and ice creams, just to name a few. For cheese making purposes in this book, it is used as a firming agent to provide textures ranging from soft to very firm.

In my first publication, The Gentle Chef Cookbook, my cheese recipes relied solely on agar as a firming agent. However, after discovering the potential of carrageenan and working with it extensively, I found it to have several advantages over agar in certain applications: Carrageenan has twice the gelling power of agar, which means a smaller amount of carrageenan is needed to produce the same firmness. By weight, carrageenan is also less expensive than agar (at least this has been my experience), which makes it more economical than using large amounts of agar to produce the same effect. Carrageenan can be activated by cooking directly in cheese mixtures, whereas agar needs to be simmered in water first to fully activate its gelling properties. Carrageenan is also heat-reversible, whereas agar is not. In other words, cheeses made with carrageenan will melt like dairy cheeses, while cheeses made with agar may soften, but they will not melt in the same manner.

I've never been able to locate carrageenan in health or natural food stores but thankfully it's available online through specialty retailers such as Modernist Pantry.

Of the three forms of carrageenan available, you will need to purchase **kappa carrageenan** to prepare the soymilk-based block cheeses in this book. Modernist Pantry offers an affordable and consistently superior quality kappa carrageenan in a home size (50 grams), for those who wish to experiment with cheese making, and a professional size (400 grams) for those who make home cheeses on a regular basis. Because carrageenan is harvested from various locations around the world and refined according to different standards by each manufacturer, I cannot guarantee the quality of kappa carrageenan purchased from other sources. Modernist Pantry also ships worldwide and is an excellent resource for obtaining high-quality agar powder, guar gum and xanthan gum too.

Please visit the Modernist Pantry website at: www.modernistpantry.com.

Disclaimer: Food-grade carrageenan is generally recognized as safe for use in cooking; however, there will be certain individuals who are sensitive to carrageenan and there have been studies done by independent researchers linking this ingredient to gastrointestinal disorders. As to the validity of these studies, it's anyone's guess.

Negative effects can be linked to just about any food or food ingredient that is consumed in excess or by individuals who are sensitive or allergic. These studies are done on small laboratory animals that are force fed large amounts of this substance over long periods of time. Frankly, that would make anyone sick. However, if you feel certain that you are sensitive to carrageenan, simply avoid it. Regrettably agar cannot be substituted for carrageenan when specified in a recipe. Fortunately, there are many other recipes to choose from that do not use this ingredient.

Cheesecloth is a woven gauze-like cotton cloth used primarily in cheese making. In non-dairy applications, it can be used in place of a nut milk bag for straining solids from plant milks. It can also be used for squeezing water from block tofu to sufficiently dry the tofu for use in various recipes.

Chipotle chili powder is made from ground whole chipotle chili peppers and has a medium Scoville value compared to other varieties, such as the milder ancho chili powder (the Scoville value is the measurement of the pungency, or spicy heat, of chili peppers). The chipotle peppers are often smoked over a wood fire, which imparts a smoky flavor mingled with their slight hint of sweetness.

Cornstarch is a familiar food thickening agent. However, in the United States it is almost always derived from genetically-modified corn. Purchase non-GMO cornstarch whenever possible or substitute with equal amounts of unmodified potato starch or arrowroot powder.

Dry sherry is a wine made primarily from Palomino grapes. It is used as a flavoring in Alpine Swiss cheese, Gruyère Melt, Sauce Fromage Blanc and Elegant Swiss Fondue. Dry sherry is very different from sweet sherry or cream sherry, so be sure to purchase the correct product. I did some research into dry sherry and found no evidence that animal products are used in its production. There is no exact flavor substitute for dry sherry, so if you cannot use this ingredient for health or ethical reasons, simply substitute with an equal amount of soymilk.

Dry white wine (e.g., Chardonnay, Sauvignon Blanc) is used as a flavoring for Jarlsberg Melt and can be used as a substitute for dry sherry in Sauce Fromage Blanc and Elegant Swiss Fondue. It has a slightly more subtle flavor than dry sherry, with fruity undertones. Regrettably, there is no exact flavor substitute for white wine, so if you cannot use this ingredient for health or ethical reasons, simply substitute with an equal amount of soymilk.

Please note that not all wineries produce wines suitable for vegans. Some wineries still use animal products, such as isinglass from fish swim bladders as a clarifying agent during the production process; and while these animal ingredients are filtered out of the finished wine, the wine is obviously not suitable for vegans. Fortunately, the list of vegan-friendly wineries is growing. Search the internet for listings or visit www.Barnivore.com.

Filtered or spring water is water that has either been purified through some form of filtration to remove chlorine and impurities or sourced and bottled from underground aquifers or pure mountain streams. Pure water is essential for producing live bacterial cultures which are used for fermenting cashew-based milk, cream and cheese; however, filtered or spring water is recommended in all recipes whether they are cultured or uncultured. Tap water filters, such as PUR™ and Brita™ are very economical and will filter large amounts of tap water effectively and conveniently.

Food processors are similar to blenders in many ways. The primary difference is that food processors use interchangeable blades and disks (attachments) instead of a fixed blade. Also, their bowls are wider and shorter, a more appropriate shape for processing solid or semi-solid foods. Usually, little or no liquid is required in the operation of the food processor, unlike a blender, which requires some amount of liquid to move the particles around the blade. However, while food processors have several advantages over blenders, they will not produce the ultra-smooth textures that high-powered blenders can achieve.

Fruit acids from white wine vinegar (acetic acid), raw apple cider vinegar (acetic acid) and lemon juice (ascorbic and citric acid), are used either alone or in combination to add flavor, acidity and tanginess to uncultured non-dairy foods. If a recipe calls for lemon juice, avoid commercial lemon juice sold in plastic "lemon" containers, as lemon oil is often added as a flavoring and this may adversely affect the flavor of the finished product.

Guar gum, also called *guaran*, is a natural substance derived from the ground seeds of the guar plant which grows primarily in Pakistan and the northern regions of India. It is used as a thickener and stabilizer in making non-dairy butter; it adds viscosity and stretch to cheese melts; and it prevents ice crystallization in ice cream. Guar gum can be purchased in some supermarkets, in most health food and natural food stores, or online through food retail websites such as Amazon.com. Substitute with xanthan gum if desired.

High-powered blenders, such as the Vitamix® or Blendtec®, are required for processing cashews and other thick ingredients such as tofu. Standard blenders simply don't have the power to churn through the ingredients used to make heavy creams and cheeses and you will quickly burn out the motor.

A bonus feature of the Vitamix™ blenders is the "tamper tool" which can be inserted through the lid. This helps keep thick mixtures turning in the blades, without having to start and stop the blender as frequently to stir.

However, one drawback to the high-powered blenders is their exorbitant price; but, as the old saying goes, "you get what you pay for". They're definitely worth the investment and will save you countless hours of time and frustration in the kitchen. I have heard that the Ninja® blender is an affordable and effective alternative; however, I haven't had the opportunity to use this appliance.

The other drawback to high-powered blenders is that the bottom doesn't unscrew from the jar, at least not with the Vitamix™. This makes retrieving thick mixtures from the bottom of the blender jar difficult. It also makes cleaning the jar more time consuming. Try using an old toothbrush to clean around the base of the blades before putting the jar in the dishwasher.

Immersion blenders, or stick blenders, are kitchen appliances that blend ingredients or purée food in the container in which they are being prepared. Immersion blenders are distinguished from standard/high-powered blenders and food processors as the latter two require the food be placed in a special container for processing. They are also distinguished from hand mixers which do not chop the food as it is blended.

Kala namak, also known as Himalayan black salt, is an Indian salt with a high mineral content, most notably sulfur, which gives it its characteristic and pungent "hard-boiled egg" smell. Oddly enough, it is pink in color when dry but turns black when moistened. It is used in eggless egg foods as it imparts a cooked egg flavor and aroma. Be advised, that if you detest the sulfurous odor of hard-boiled eggs, you probably will not care for this salt. Kala namak is considered a cooling spice in Ayurvedic medicine and is used as a digestive aid. It can be found in specialty food stores as well as though the internet. Himalayan pink salt is not the same thing, so this can make purchasing rather confusing since kala namak is also pink when dry. Specifically look for the names *kala namak* or *Himalayan black salt*.

Lecithin (Organic Soy), simply stated, is a natural, waxy substance derived from the processing of organic soybeans. It is an essential ingredient for promoting the emulsification of soymilk and oil when making non-dairy butter; in other words, it binds the oil and soymilk together. Organic soy lecithin can be purchased in granule, powder or liquid syrup forms and can be found in most health food and natural food stores, or online through food retail websites such as Amazon.com. Sunflower lecithin, which is derived from sunflower seeds, can be substituted.

Liquid soy lecithin is very sticky and can be rather difficult to remove from measuring utensils. Coat the inside of the measuring spoon with a small amount of the melted coconut oil or vegetable oil before measuring to reduce adhesion to the spoon. Wipe the spoon with a paper towel to remove the excess residue and then wash with hot, soapy water by hand or in an automatic dishwasher. The food processor or immersion blender, and any other utensils used to make butter, will also need to be thoroughly washed in this manner as well. Consider using dry lecithin granules or powder for easier cleanup.

Mellow white miso paste is a Japanese seasoning produced by the fermentation of soybeans (or chickpeas or barley) with salt and the fungus, *kōjikin* (*aspergillis oryzae*). It is used as a culturing and flavoring ingredient in non-dairy cheese, sauces, melts and fondue. Miso adds *umami* (a Japanese word used to describe a pleasant savory flavor) and also contributes to the "ripened" flavor of the cheese. Mellow white miso paste can be found in natural food markets and health food stores in the refrigerator section. It has a very long refrigerator shelf life, usually about 2 years.

Mustard in dry, ground powder form is a flavoring spice. However, in some recipes it serves a dual purpose as a flavoring ingredient and an emulsifier. The coating of the mustard seed contains a fair amount of mucilage (a thick, sticky substance) which helps to coat molecules of oil, allowing them to coexist harmoniously with watery substances. In mayonnaise, for example, it helps the oil and soymilk bind together. If dry ground mustard is specified in a recipe, do not omit, as it was included for a reason.

Nut milk bags are made from ultra-fine nylon mesh (similar to the weave of nylon stockings). They are very effective for straining extremely fine solids from nut, seed and grain milks and for straining the okara (pulp) from soymilk. They are also economical as they can be washed and reused repeatedly (as opposed to cheesecloth).

To use the bag, first wash your hands thoroughly. Hold the bag at the top and place it over a large bowl or measuring cup. Pour in the milk or cream and with your other hand gently massage and squeeze the bag to press the liquid through the mesh. Turn the bag inside out to rinse and discard or compost the solids. Wash with unscented natural dish soap in hot water, rinse well and lay flat on a clean dish towel to dry.

A large strainer lined with 4 layers of cheesecloth will work in a similar manner, except the milk or cream will need to be stirred with a spoon to help the liquid pass though the cheesecloth. Nut milk bags can sometimes be found in health food or natural food stores but can easily be found online. *TheRawFoodWorld.com* offers high-quality nut milk bags.

Nutritional yeast is an ingredient used extensively as a flavoring and coloring agent in non-dairy cheese and eggless egg foods. Nutritional yeast is a non-active form of yeast and has a very cheese-like flavor. It is naturally low in fat and sodium and is free of sugar and dairy. Bob's Red Mill™ produces a superior quality, vitamin-fortified nutritional yeast with a rich golden color. Nutritional yeast can be found in most health and natural food stores or online through food retail websites such as Amazon.com.

Organic refined coconut oil provides the solid fat essential for thickening cashew-based sour cream and cultured cheeses; for firming tofu-based cheeses; and for creating the proper texture and melting properties in the soy-milk based block cheeses. In many respects, it shares striking similarities to dairy butterfat, but without the cholesterol (and animal exploitation). Coconut oil, like butterfat, also becomes semi-solid at room temperature and very solid when chilled, therefore it must be melted for proper measurement in recipes. This can be done by removing the metal lid from the jar and placing the jar into a microwave to heat for 30 seconds to 1 minute (depending upon the solidity of the coconut oil). Avoid overheating the oil, especially when preparing cultured foods. Alternately, the jar can be placed in about an inch of simmering water and melted in the same manner. Repeated melting and re-chilling of the oil will not harm it in any way.

The amount of coconut oil used in the recipes has been carefully formulated to produce the proper results. Although it may be tempting to reduce or eliminate the oil for health and weight control purposes, this is not recommended. The creams will not thicken properly and the cheeses will not have the proper texture. It is much better to moderate your consumption of non-dairy foods than to tamper with the recipes.

The best creams and cheeses, whether dairy or non-dairy, must contain fat for flavor and texture. If you've ever had low-fat dairy cheese in the past, you'll know exactly what I mean - it's dry, flavorless and does not melt well. Dairy cheese contains between 30% to 45% butterfat for low-fat varieties and upwards of 50% for regular varieties (in some cases as high as 80%). The non-dairy cheeses in this book, on average, contain between 25% to 33% plant fat. So, compared to dairy cheese, they remain well within or below the low-fat range.

Virgin organic coconut oil is not recommended for making butter, sour cream or cheese. While in most cases I would always recommend less refined or less processed ingredients, this is not the case when it comes to coconut oil used in most non-dairy foods - unless you're okay with your butter, sour cream and cheese having a distinct coconut undertaste. Refining removes the coconut flavor and aroma from coconut oil and therefore is a better option. Save the virgin coconut oil for desserts.

De-scented organic cocoa butter has properties similar to coconut oil and could potentially be used as a replacement (which would be a good option for those allergic to coconuts). However, it is not available to me locally and is very expensive through the internet; therefore I haven't had the opportunity to experiment with it at this time.

Organic refined coconut oil can be found in many larger supermarket chains, health food stores and natural food stores or purchased online through food retail websites.

Organic sugar is made from organic sugar cane. The juice is pressed from organic raw sugar cane, evaporated and then crushed into crystals. In adherence with strict Organic Standards, the fields are green cut and not burned or treated with herbicides or synthetic fertilizers. No chemicals or animal by-products are used to decolorize the sugar. This makes it very different from refined white sugar, which has been decolorized by filtering through animal bone char.

Plain unsweetened soymilk is used as a base for the block cheeses in this book. Soymilk, of all the plant milks available, is the closest to dairy milk in composition. More importantly, it emulsifies successfully with plant fat when cooked (in other words it binds together with the coconut oil to make cheese). It is essential to use soymilk that is free of additives, specifically gums, starches, gels (such as carrageenan) and sweeteners, as these ingredients will adversely affect the recipe results. Vitamin and calcium fortified soymilk, however, is acceptable and will not affect recipe results.

Westsoy™ produces a high quality unsweetened, organic, non-GMO and additive-free soymilk. Homemade soymilk is the best option if commercial additive-free soymilk is unavailable. However, it must be thoroughly strained to remove as much of the okara (pulp) as possible; if not, the cheeses will have a pasty "mouthfeel" and texture when melted. Detailed instructions are provided with the recipe for Plain Unsweetened Soymilk on page 14.

Rejuvelac is a non-alcoholic fermented liquid made from grain. In this book, it serves as a culturing agent for fermenting cashew milk and cashew cream, which in turn is used for producing the finest cultured non-dairy buttermilk, sour cream and cashew-based cheeses. Lactic acid is the by-product of fermentation with Rejuvelac and this acid is what creates the sour, tangy or "sharp" flavor in cultured non-dairy foods. In cheeses, this flavor intensifies and develops secondary flavor characteristics during "ripening".

Cultured non-dairy foods are a health benefit to those adhering to a plant-based diet, which is often lacking in cultured foods. These "friendly" bacteria help contribute to a healthy intestinal flora, which keeps harmful pathogens in check and also assists in the absorption of nutrients.

Tapioca flour, also known as tapioca starch, is a carbohydrate extracted from the cassava plant (*Manihot esculenta*). It is used worldwide as a thickening agent in foods. It differs from wheat flour, potato starch, and cornstarch or arrowroot powder in that it produces a gooey, stretchy texture when heated in liquids. This makes it an ideal thickener for producing cheeses, cheese melts, cheese sauces and fondues. Tapioca flour can be purchased in some supermarkets, in most health food and natural food stores, or online through food retail websites such as Amazon.com.

Tofu, or bean curd, is made from soymilk that has been coagulated and pressed into soft white blocks. It is of Chinese origin, and is also a part of East Asian and Southeast Asian cuisine such as Chinese, Japanese, Korean, Indonesian, Vietnamese, and others.

Tofu is considered a staple in plant-based diets, because of its high protein content, low content of calories and fat, high calcium and iron content and the ability to substitute for eggs in a variety of recipes. Tofu has a subtle flavor and can be used in both savory recipes and desserts.

Calcium sulfate (gypsum) is the traditional and most widely used coagulant to produce water-packed block tofu. The resulting tofu curd is tender yet firm in texture and the coagulant itself has no perceivable taste. Use of this coagulant also produces a tofu that is rich in calcium. The coagulant and soymilk are mixed together in large vats, allowed to curdle and the resulting curds are drained, pressed into blocks and then packaged.

Water-packed block tofu is sold in plastic tub containers completely immersed in water to maintain its moisture content and it will always be found in the refrigerated section of the market. It ranges in density and texture from soft to extra-firm. Soft to firm water-packed block tofu is recommended for eggless scrambles, as this form of tofu holds up better to "scrambling" than silken tofu which, in my opinion, is too delicate in texture. Extra-firm water-packed block tofu is used for making tofu-based cheeses.

The recipes in this book will specify whether to use a block of soft to firm or extra-firm water-packed tofu or whether to use a carton of firm or extra-firm silken tofu. It is essential to know the difference, as the type of tofu used will definitely affect your cooking results.

Silken tofu, because of its delicate texture and neutral flavor, is used for a variety of cooked eggless egg foods such as sunnyside-ups, omelettes, frittatas and quiches. It's also used as an egg replacement in desserts, since it has a smoother and more custard-like texture compared to the firmer, water-packed block tofu. Magnesium chloride and calcium chloride are the coagulants (called *nigari* in Japan) used to make silken tofu. These coagulants are added to soymilk and the mixture is then sealed in 12.3 oz. aseptic cartons. In other words, the resulting bean curd is produced inside its own package, rather than being drained and pressed into blocks.

Silken tofu packaged in this manner needs no refrigeration until the carton is opened. This gives it an extended shelf life, compared to fresh water-packed tofu sold in tub containers.

However, silken tofu can now also be found in 1 lb. tub containers in the refrigerated section next to the firmer water-packed block tofu. This can be somewhat confusing if you're new to tofu, so it's important to read labels and be aware of what you're purchasing.

Whenever a recipe calls for silken tofu, it's referring to the 12.3 oz. silken tofu packaged in the aseptic carton. If you purchase silken tofu in a 1 lb. refrigerated tub container, you will have to weigh the tofu before using in the recipe.

Preparing Tofu for Recipes

To prepare silken tofu for the recipes in this book, open the carton with kitchen shears and drain any small amount of liquid inside. Carefully slide the tofu from the carton and place on several layers of paper towels or a clean, smooth kitchen towel lining a plate (do not use terry cloth because the tofu may pick up lint). Set aside for about 20 minutes or until the excess moisture has been absorbed into the towel(s). You will be surprised how much liquid is absorbed. Avoid applying any significant pressure to the tofu as it will crumble very easily; gentle blotting will suffice. The tofu can also be cut into slabs as directed in a recipe and drained in the same manner.

To prepare water-packed block tofu for the recipes in this book, remove the tofu from its container and discard the liquid. Slice the tofu into 4 to 6 pieces and place on a plate lined with several layers of paper towels or a clean, smooth kitchen towel (do not use terry cloth because the tofu may pick up lint). Cover with additional towels and place a cutting board on top of the towels. Now place something heavy (like a cast-iron skillet) on top of the cutting board. Allow to press for about 30 minutes. This should sufficiently remove the excess moisture and the tofu will be ready for your recipe.

For recipes calling for crumbled block tofu, the water can also be effectively pressed by first slicing the tofu and then wrapping the slices in 2 or 3 layers of cheesecloth or a clean, lint-free kitchen towel (make sure there is enough to completely enclose the tofu). Twist the top of the bundle securely closed, and then twist and squeeze the enclosed tofu to drain the liquid into the kitchen sink. The tofu will now be sufficiently dry to use in the recipe. This is the best method when preparing tofu for tofu-based cheeses, as it thoroughly and completely removes any residual water.

The tofu press is a spring-loaded device which also presses water effectively from a standard-size block of commercially made water-packed tofu. No more excessive paper towel waste!

However, it has been my experience that the press is not as effective for removing water from silken tofu, even when using the lighter tension spring supplied with the press. Visit the TofuXpress.com website directly to learn more about their product.

The Tofu Press

Tomato paste is an ingredient used in varying amounts to add a warm golden color to cheddar-style cheeses, melts and sauces. Look for tube tomato paste in the pasta sauce, gourmet section or spice section of your market (it's packaged like a tube of toothpaste). It stays fresh in the refrigerator much longer than canned tomato paste, which needs to be transferred to a small storage container after the can has been opened.

Unmodified potato starch is one of the less familiar starches used as a food thickener. It can be used in equal amounts as an alternate to cornstarch or arrowroot powder. Bob's Red Mill™ produces a high-quality and inexpensive unmodified potato starch.

Vegetable oil, when specified in a recipe, refers to any plant oil with a mild taste such as organic soybean, safflower, sunflower, grapeseed or mild-tasting olive oil (avoid extra-virgin olive oil for making butter or mayonnaise because of its strong flavor).

Whole raw cashews are ideal for making milk and cream because of their perfect balance of sweetness and mild flavor. The milk, cream and emulsion derived from cashews makes an excellent medium for culturing buttermilk, sour cream, yogurt and cashew-based cheeses because cashews contain the ideal amount of natural sugar to feed the beneficial bacterial strains, with no additional sugar required. The natural sugar in the cashews is converted by the bacteria into lactic acid which produces the characteristic sour, tangy or sharp flavor of cultured products. If possible, avoid purchasing cashew halves and pieces because they are often dried out (lacking in natural moisture or oils). It is essential to soak the cashew nuts in water for a minimum of 8 hours to soften them before processing, so plan accordingly. I purchase raw cashews in bulk through Amazon.com.

Storage Life of Non-Dairy Foods

Better Butter will stay fresh for several weeks in the refrigerator and can be stored in the freezer for up to 3 months.

Fresh cashew milk has a brief refrigerator shelf life of only 3 to 4 days. However, fresh rice milk and soymilk will last about a week. Try pouring any non-dairy milk that will not be consumed within a few days into ice cube trays, freeze and then store in freezer bags for quick use later.

Non-cultured cheeses have a limit of about 2 weeks; although vacuum-sealing the cheeses will extend their shelf life considerably. They can also be frozen for up to 3 months. The recommended limit for cultured foods is 3 to 4 weeks. Cultured foods should not be frozen.

Eggless egg foods and prepared desserts (other than ice cream, of course) have a refrigerated storage limit of 7 to 10 days.

There are no hard and fast rules, however, and these are only rough guidelines. My best advice is to use your own judgment. Obviously, if something is moldy, or smells "off" or tastes odd, then it's time to discard.

Butter, Milks and Creams

Better Butter

Better Butter is a superior tasting, palm oil-free alternative to dairy butter and commercial non-dairy margarine. This recipe produces a butter that looks, tastes and melts like dairy butter and can be used in any recipe, including baking, as you would dairy butter.

Just like its dairy counterpart, melted Better Butter browns and burns when exposed to high heat and therefore should not be used for high-heat sautéing - it works best with low to medium heat.

The best tools for emulsifying the butter ingredients are a food processor or an immersion blender. The ingredients can also be emulsified using a standard or high-speed blender; however, retrieving the thick butter from around the blades can be difficult. This recipe yields about 2 cups of butter.

Ingredients:

- 1 cup organic refined coconut oil
- ⅓ cup mild vegetable oil
- ⅔ cup plain unsweetened soymilk with no additives (sorry, no substitutes)
- 2 tsp raw apple cider vinegar
- 1 tsp organic sugar
- 4 tsp organic liquid soy lecithin or 3 T organic dry lecithin granules
- ½ tsp sea salt (for sweet cream butter, omit the salt)
- ½ tsp nutritional yeast
- ½ tsp guar gum or xanthan gum

Technique:

You will need a 2 cup minimum food storage container with a lid to store the butter. If you prefer, the butter can be shaped in a flexible silicone form, or divided into several forms, and released after hardening.

First, remove the metal lid from the jar of coconut oil and place the jar in a microwave. Heat just until the solid oil liquefies, about 30 seconds to 1 minute (this will depend upon the solidity of the coconut oil).

Alternately, you can place the jar in about an inch of simmering water and melt the oil in the same manner. Pour 1 cup of the coconut oil into a 2-cup measuring cup or other suitable container with a pouring "lip". Add ⅓ cup vegetable oil to the coconut oil and set aside.

Food processor method:

Add the remaining ingredients to the processor and turn on the processor. Now begin to pour the mixed oils into the mixture through the food chute. Continue to process until the mixture is emulsified and thick. Transfer to a sealable container, cover and freeze until solid (if using one or several silicone molds, cover with plastic wrap).

Immersion blender method:

Add the remaining ingredients to a 4-cup glass measuring cup or heavy glass/ceramic bowl. Insert the immersion blender and process the mixture for about 15 seconds.

Now, with the immersion blender running on high speed, begin pouring the mixed oils into the blending cup or bowl. Move the blender up and down and side to side as you add the oils. Continue blending until the mixture is emulsified and thick. Transfer to a sealable container, cover and freeze until solid (if using one or several silicone molds, cover with plastic wrap).

Freezing is important, as it prevents the mixture from separating. Once frozen, place the butter in the refrigerator until thawed before using; or it can be stored in the freezer for up to 3 months. To release the butter from a form, simply wiggle the sides a bit to loosen and then press out onto a plate.

Ghee

Ghee is prepared from Better Butter that has been melted and simmered until all of the moisture has been removed, thus separating the solids from the fat. The butter takes on a browned, nutty flavor which is especially favored in Indian cuisine.

Ingredients:

- a minimum of 1 cup Better Butter (pg. 12)

Technique:

Place the butter in a small saucepan and melt over medium-low heat. Let the mixture simmer undisturbed for 5 minutes. Remove from the heat and let cool for 10 minutes. Pour through a fine mesh strainer into a sealable container and refrigerate for up to 4 months.

Plain Unsweetened Soymilk

Soymilk is a beverage made from soybeans. A traditional staple of Asian cuisine, it is a stable emulsion of oil, water, and protein (meaning it does not separate). Soymilk is produced by soaking dry soybeans, grinding them in water, straining out the solid pulp and then cooking the milk. Soy milk contains about the same proportion of protein as cow's milk: around 3.5%, along with 2% fat and 2.9% carbohydrates.

Commercial soymilks often contain additional ingredients for both thickening and sweetening. This recipe produces a pure soymilk free of additives which is essential for the soymilk-based cheeses, melts and sauces in this book. Of course, for drinking palatability you can add the optional sea salt and organic sugar. Always purchase organic non-GMO soybeans (we don't want to support Monsanto). "Laura" soybeans are a specific variety of soybeans that produce a mild milk.

This recipe yields 4 cups or 1 quart of fresh soymilk. For 2 quarts of fresh soymilk, simply double the recipe and process and strain the raw milk in 2 separate batches before cooking. Fresh soymilk has a limited refrigerator storage life, so if you can't consume the milk within 7 days, freeze the prepared milk in ice cube trays and store the cubes in zip-lock bags for later use.

Ingredients:

- ½ cup dry organic non-GMO soybeans
- 4 cups water
- ½ tsp sea salt (optional; omit for cheese making)
- a pinch of ground ginger* (optional)
- 2 T organic sugar (optional for drinking palatability; omit for cheese making)

*Ground ginger helps reduce the rather distinct soybean aroma of the milk, which some find unpleasant, but is purely an optional ingredient. Any flavor of ginger will be imperceptible in the milk.

You will also need a high-powered blender, and a nut milk bag to strain the okara (pulp) from the milk. A large strainer lined with 4 layers of cheesecloth and a large spoon can be used in place of the nut milk bag.

Rinse the beans in a strainer to make sure they are clean, then put them in a mason jar (home canning jar) or other suitable container and fill with cold water (about 3 cups). Refrigerate for a minimum of 8 hours, 12 hours being ideal. After soaking, drain the water from the beans, discarding the soaking water.

Place the beans into a high-powered blender with 4 cups of fresh water, the optional salt and the optional pinch of ginger powder. Process the contents on high speed for 2 full minutes.

The raw milk will now need to be strained to remove the solids. To do this, wash your hands thoroughly and pour the milk into the nut milk bag over a large cooking pot.

While holding the top of the bag with one hand, firmly knead and squeeze the bag with your other hand to help the milk pass through the fine mesh and to extract as much of the milk as you can from the pulp. This may take several minutes, so be patient.

Optionally, place the strainer lined with cheesecloth over the cooking pot and pour the milk (in increments) into the strainer. Stir the milk with a large spoon to help it pass through the cheesecloth.

Discard or compost the okara (pulp) in the bag or cheesecloth.

Now place the pot over high heat to bring to a rapid simmer. Stir continually to prevent the soymilk from scorching on the bottom of the cooking pot. As the soymilk begins to come to a rapid simmer, immediately reduce the heat to medium-low. Reducing the heat is very important, as rapid boiling may cause the soymilk to rise in volume and boil over the top of the pot. Continue to stir the soymilk and cook for 5 minutes.

While simmering, lightly skim any foam from the surface of the soymilk and discard. The foam contains the compounds (oligosaccharides) responsible for causing excess intestinal gas.

After 5 minutes, remove the pot from the heat, cover and let cool for about 30 minutes. Add the optional sugar at this time and stir well to dissolve.

After 30 minutes, skim off any "skin" that has formed on the surface of the milk and discard. If you will be using the soymilk for making any of the cheeses, melts or sauces in this book (or you simply prefer an extra-smooth milk), ladle the milk into the nut milk bag over a large pitcher or other suitable container and repeat the straining process without squeezing the milk through the mesh material. This will help capture additional micro-fine particles. Discard or compost the residual okara.

Transfer the milk to a sealable container and refrigerate.

Whole Rice Milk

Whole rice milk is made from brown rice and is especially useful for those with sensitivities to soy or nuts. It's higher in carbohydrates than soy or cashew milk and has a rather distinct (but not unpleasant) starchy flavor. When lightly sweetened, it is very palatable for drinking and is especially good for pouring over cold cereal. Rice milk is ideal for making Horchata (pg. 139), a sweetened Latin American beverage flavored with cinnamon and vanilla. This recipe yields about 4 cups or 1 quart.

Fresh rice milk has a limited refrigerator storage life, so if you can't consume 1 quart within 7 days, freeze the prepared milk in ice cube trays and store the cubes in zip-lock bags for later use.

Ingredients:

- ⅓ cup organic long grain brown rice
- 4 and ½ cups water
- 2 T organic sugar
- 1 T sunflower or safflower oil
- ½ tsp sea salt (omit for sodium-free diets)

You will also need a blender, cooking tongs and a nut milk bag to strain any residual solids from the milk. A fine mesh strainer lined with 4 layers of cheesecloth and a large spoon can be used in place of the nut milk bag and cooking tongs.

Technique:

Rinse the rice thoroughly in a strainer and add to a large saucepan. Add the water, sugar, oil and optional salt and bring to a rapid boil. Stir, cover and reduce the heat to low. Cook for 45 minutes. Let the rice mixture cool for about 30 minutes before proceeding.

Pour the rice mixture into a blender, put the lid in place and cover the lid with a dish towel (to prevent steam burns). Start the blender on low speed, slowly increasing to high speed and process for 2 full minutes. Let the mixture cool for about 30 minutes.

The milk will now need to be strained to remove the rice solids. Pour the milk into the nut milk bag over a large bowl or pitcher. The milk will still be hot, so cooking tongs will come in handy for the next step.

While holding the top of the bag with one hand, gently squeeze the bag repeatedly with the tongs to help press the milk through the ultra-fine mesh. Optionally, the milk can be poured into a strainer lined with 4 layers of cheesecloth that has been placed over a large bowl or pitcher. Stir the milk with a large spoon to help it pass through the cheesecloth. Transfer the milk to a sealable container and refrigerate. Shake well before using.

Whole Raw Cashew Milk

Commercial nut milks can be purchased easily enough, but these milks usually include a significant amount of sugar, stabilizers, thickeners and sometimes preservatives. Many varieties of nuts and seeds can be used to make milk, but in my opinion whole raw cashews produce the mildest, creamiest milk with just the right amount of natural sweetness that additional sweeteners are generally unnecessary. However, if you've adapted to commercial non-dairy milks with sweeteners, this milk may taste a bit bland and a natural sweetener can always be added to suit your taste.

This recipe yields about 4 cups or 1 quart of whole raw cashew milk. Raw cashew milk has a brief refrigerator storage life, so if you can't consume 1 quart within 3 to 4 days, freeze the prepared milk in ice cube trays and store the cubes in zip-lock bags for later use.

Ingredients:

- 1 cup (5 oz. by weight) whole raw cashews
- 4 cups water
- ½ tsp sea salt (optional)
- 4 tsp organic sugar, or more to taste (optional)

You will also need a high-powered blender and a nut milk bag or fine mesh strainer lined with 4 layers of cheesecloth to strain any residual solids from the milk.

Technique:

Soak the nuts for a minimum of 8 hours in the refrigerator with enough water to cover. Drain the nuts, discarding the soaking water. Add the nuts to a high-powered blender with 4 cups of fresh water and the optional salt. Process the mixture on high speed for 2 full minutes.

The milk will now need to be strained to remove the solids. To do this, wash your hands thoroughly and then pour the milk into the nut milk bag over a large bowl or pitcher. While holding the top of the bag with one hand, gently knead and squeeze the bag to help the milk pass through the ultra-fine mesh.

Optionally, the milk can be poured (in increments) into a strainer lined with 4 layers of cheesecloth. Stir the milk gently with a spoon to help it pass through the cheesecloth.

Discard or compost the solids in the bag or cheesecloth.

For an extra-smooth milk, repeat the straining process without squeezing the bag. This will help capture additional micro-fine particles. Sweeten the milk to taste if desired. Transfer the milk to a sealable container and refrigerate. Cashew milk has a tendency to separate, so shake well before using.

Heavy Cream and Light Cream

Cream is made by processing cashew nuts with non-dairy milk. The mixture is then strained to remove the solids, which produces a velvety smooth texture. Heavy cream is the ideal substitute for any recipe calling for heavy dairy cream. It's an essential ingredient for non-dairy cream soups (cream of mushroom, cream of broccoli, etc.) and is wonderful for adding creaminess to mashed potatoes. Light cream can be used in any recipe calling for light dairy cream. This recipe yields about 2 cups of the finest heavy or light cream which should be sufficient for most recipes.

Ingredients for heavy cream:

- 1 cup (5 oz. by weight) whole raw cashews
- 2 cups non-dairy milk of your choice
- ¼ tsp sea salt

Ingredients for light cream:

- ½ cup (2.5 oz. by weight) whole raw cashews
- 2 cups non-dairy milk of your choice
- ¼ tsp sea salt

Technique:

Place the cashews and milk into a container with a lid, seal and place in the refrigerator to soak for a minimum of 8 hours. After soaking, place the ingredients in a high-powered blender with the optional salt and process on high speed for 2 full minutes.

The cream will now need to be strained to remove the solids. To do this, wash your hands thoroughly and pour the cream into the nut milk bag over a large bowl or pitcher.

While holding the top of the bag with one hand, gently knead the bag to help the cream pass through the ultra-fine mesh - avoid forcing the cream through. Discard or compost the solids in the bag.

Optionally, the cream can be poured (in increments) into a strainer lined with 4 layers of cheesecloth. Stir the cream gently with a spoon to help it pass through the cheesecloth. Transfer the cream to a sealable container and refrigerate. Cream has a tendency to separate, so shake well before using.

Coffee and Tea Creamer

This recipe yields about 2 cups of velvety smooth and naturally sweetened coffee or tea creamer.

Ingredients:

- 2 cups plain or vanilla non-dairy milk
- ½ cup (2.5 oz. by weight) whole raw cashews
- 6 pitted dates

You will also need a high-powered blender and a nut milk bag or a fine mesh strainer lined with 4 layers of cheesecloth to strain the solids from the cream.

*For mocha creamer, use chocolate non-dairy milk. For unsweetened creamer, follow the recipe for Light Cream on page 18.

Technique:

Combine the milk, nuts and dates into a container with a lid, seal and place in the refrigerator to soak for a minimum of 8 hours. After soaking, place the ingredients in a blender and process on high speed for 2 full minutes.

Coffee and tea creamer requires a very smooth texture, so the cream will now need to be finely strained. To do this, wash your hands thoroughly and then pour the cream into the nut milk bag over a large bowl or pitcher.

While holding the top of the bag with one hand, gently knead the bag to help the cream pass through the ultra-fine mesh - avoid forcing the cream through. Discard or compost the solids in the bag.

Optionally, the cream can be poured (in increments) into a strainer lined with 4 layers of cheesecloth. Stir the cream with a spoon to help it pass through the cheesecloth.

Transfer the cream to a sealable container and refrigerate. Shake well before using.

Chai Thai Iced Tea

This refreshing beverage is a unique variation of the popular sweetened iced tea served in Thai restaurants. Chai is a South Asian flavored tea beverage made by brewing black tea with a mixture of aromatic Indian herbs and spices. The black tea infusion itself is less concentrated than the tea used for making traditional Thai iced tea. The layers of date-sweetened cream and fragrant and sweet Chai tea make a lovely presentation. This recipe serves 2.

Ingredients:

- 6 teabags of Ceylon black tea (or any strong black tea) (decaffeinated if you prefer, or a combination of both)
- 1 and ½ cup boiling water
- 1 thin slice of fresh ginger root
- 1 piece star anise (or ½ tsp fennel or anise seed)
- 2 whole cloves
- 2 pods green cardamom
- 2 black peppercorns
- ½ stick cinnamon
- 1 T organic sugar, or more to taste
- crushed ice
- Coffee and Tea Creamer (pg. 19)
- mint leaves for garnish (optional)

Simple version:

- 6 teabags of spiced chai tea (such as Bigelow's Spiced Chai Tea ™) (decaffeinated if you prefer, or a combination of both)
- 1 and ½ cup boiling water
- 1 T organic sugar, or more to taste
- crushed ice
- Coffee and Tea Creamer (pg. 19)
- mint leaves for garnish (optional)

Technique:

Steep the teabags and spices in the boiling hot water until cooled. Add the sugar while the tea is still warm and stir to dissolve.

Add 2 to 3 tablespoons of creamer to the bottom of each glass. Fill the glasses with crushed ice and then strain ¾ cup of tea into each glass. Serve with the optional mint garnish.

Heavenly Whipped Cream

This heavenly whipped topping rivals its finest dairy counterpart. Smooth, creamy, lightly sweetened and flavored with a hint of vanilla, it's ideal for topping non-dairy desserts. Follow the instructions to the letter and you will have success every time. Enjoy, but consume moderately - this is not a low fat/calorie topping! This recipe yields about 2 cups of whipped cream.

Ingredients:

- 1 and ½ cup solid coconut cream*
- ⅓ cup organic sugar
- ½ tsp real vanilla extract

Special equipment needed:

- a ceramic or metal mixing bowl (ceramic is ideal because it stays cold longer)
- an electric beater
- a mini or standard blender

*Coconut cream is the solid fat that rises to the top of full-fat coconut milk when chilled. "Creamed coconut" and "cream of coconut" are not the same product, as they often contain sugar and additional ingredients including fragments of coconut meat. Coconut manna is also a different "whole food" coconut product - in other words, it contains the coconut meat as well as the cream.

The amount of coconut cream in coconut milk will vary from brand to brand and even from can to can. Look for the words "first-pressing" on the can, as this is usually a good indicator (but not always) that the can will contain more coconut cream. Two 13.5 oz. cans of organic, unsweetened, full-fat coconut milk should yield enough cream for this recipe. However, depending upon the yield of the brand you are using, you may need additional cans. I have had the most consistent amount of coconut cream per can using Native Forest™ organic coconut milk.

Technique:

Chill the cans of coconut milk towards the back of the refrigerator for a minimum of 48 hours. The cans must get as cold as possible without freezing. This will ensure that the cream is completely solidified and separated from the coconut water.

Place your mixing bowl and the metal beaters in the freezer to get VERY cold.

Place ⅓ cup organic sugar and ½ tsp cornstarch (preferably non-GMO) in a dry blender. Pulse process until the sugar is finely powdered.* Set aside.

Now open the top of the cans with a can opener, leaving a small hinge for the lids to stay attached. Scoop out the solidified cream until you reach the coconut water and place in the mixing bowl. If using a good quality coconut milk, there should be a substantial amount of cream. Close the lid and drain away the coconut water, reserving for another use if desired (smoothies perhaps?) DO NOT add the coconut water to the mixing bowl!

Open the can and scoop out any remaining cream that may have solidified near the bottom of the can (if any) and add to the mixing bowl. Add the vanilla and powdered sugar to the cream and fold in to combine.

Beat the mixture on high-speed for several minutes until the mixture is thick, smooth and peaks begin to form. Transfer to an air-tight container and refrigerate until ready to use. The whipped cream will stay firm as long as it is refrigerated.

Cultured Milks and Creams

Rejuvelac

Rejuvelac is a non-alcoholic fermented liquid made from sprouted grains. It is an inexpensive and easy-to-make probiotic rich in lactobacilli, nutrients and enzymes. Drinking a small amount each day is very beneficial to the digestive system, promoting a healthy intestinal flora. However, in this book it is specifically used to culture cashew milk and cashew cream for producing the finest non-dairy buttermilk, sour cream, and cashew-based cheeses.

Rejuvelac can be prepared using many different types of grain, but I use organic white wheat berries (raw wheat) and the process works perfectly every time. You may come across different varieties of wheat when shopping for wheat berries, such as hard or soft; red or white; or Spring or Winter. For the best results, purchase organic soft white wheat berries or organic soft white Spring wheat berries (they're actually gold in color). If you choose to work with a different grain, do some internet research on preparing rejuvelac with that particular grain, as soaking and preparation times may be different.

So exactly how does this process work? Prior to its decay, plant material begins to ferment (a bacterial ferment, not an alcoholic ferment). When the sprouted grain sits in standing water, an anaerobic environment (lack of oxygen) occurs and the lactobacillus bacteria, which are present everywhere in the environment around us, begin to grow.

Lactobacillus is a genus of anaerobic rod-shaped bacteria. "Lacto" refers to their ability to convert lactose and other sugars to lactic acid. Eventually the bacteria produce so much acid that decay bacteria cannot survive. Lactic acid is the compound responsible for souring milk and producing sharp flavors in cheese. Various strains of lactobacillus are also used for the production of yogurt, sauerkraut, pickles, beer, wine, hard cider, kimchi, cocoa, and other fermented foods.

Rejuvelac has a mild, yeast-like aroma and a tart, lemony flavor. Organic wheat berries can usually be found in health or natural food stores, or purchased online through food retail websites such as Amazon.com. Preparation can take anywhere from 3 to 6 days (depending on ambient room temperature), so plan accordingly and always keep plenty of Rejuvelac on hand.

To prepare Rejuvelac, you will need:

- 1 cup dry organic soft white wheat berries
- filtered or spring water – DO NOT use tap water!
- 2 one-quart mason jars (home canning jars)
- 2 squares of double layered cheesecloth and 2 lid rings
  or 2 stainless steel or plastic sprouting lids (available in health foods stores or through the internet)

Technique:

First, before you begin, it is important that anything that comes into contact with the grain (your hands, utensils and containers) be washed thoroughly to prevent contamination of the culture. Cleanliness ensures efficient culturing of the grain (in other words, the lactobacillus bacteria will not have to compete with undesirable organisms).

To make 6 cups of Rejuvelac, place 1 cup whole wheat berries in a clean mason jar and fill with filtered or spring water. Do not use tap water as it may contain traces of chlorine which prevent fermentation. Swirl the contents, let the grains settle to the bottom and carefully pour off the water from the jar. Repeat the rinsing process with filtered or spring water.

Now fill the jar with filtered or spring water again, place a square of double-layer cheesecloth over the mouth of the jar and screw the lid ring in place or use a sprouting lid. Let the grains soak at room temperature for 12 hours.

After 12 hours, thoroughly drain and discard the water by pouring through the cheesecloth or sprouting lid. Turn the jar on its side and gently shake to distribute the grains along the bottom. Place the jar in an area that will receive light during the day, but out of direct sunlight.

Twice a day for 2 to 3 days, add filtered or spring water to the jar through the cheesecloth or sprouting lid, swirl, pour out the water and again, shake to distribute the grains on the bottom and set the jar on its side. In the warmer Summer months, rinse four times a day. You should see little tails emerging from the grains on the second or third day. There is no need to let the grains sprout further; proceed to the next step.

Once the little tails have appeared on a large percentage of the grain, rinse a final time with filtered or spring water. Now pour approximately half the grain from the one jar into the second jar. Fill each jar with 3 cups of filtered or spring water. Place a fresh square of cheesecloth over the mouth of each jar and secure with the lid rings (or cover with the sprouting lids).

Set the jars in an upright position, ideally in a cool, dark place. Fermentation will take anywhere from 24 to 72 hours at room temperature.

The ideal temperature for fermentation is between 68°F to 70°F. At temperatures over 70°F, fermentation begins to accelerate and there is a risk of pathogenic bacteria overrunning the culture before the lactobacillus bacteria has had a chance to populate. At temperatures under 60°F, fermentation may not occur at all.

I have had the best results with fermentation during the cooler Autumn, Winter and early Spring months. During cooler weather, the Rejuvelac can ferment for the full 72 hours without becoming rancid. Longer fermentation at cooler temperatures produces a more potent Rejuvelac with less chance of rancidity. In the later Spring and Summer months however, even when the house feels comfortable, the Rejuvelac ferments much quicker, usually within 24 to 36 hours and there is still a risk of rancidity. Therefore, to reduce the risk of spoilage, place the jars in the coolest area of your home during fermentation.

The liquid will turn cloudy as the grain ferments. If you agitate the jars gently, you will notice gas bubbles rising from the grain. This is carbon dioxide being released as a by-product of fermentation. Foam may also collect near the surface during fermentation. This is normal.

Check the jars every 24 hours and smell the mixture through the cheesecloth or lid. After 24 to 72 hours, the resulting culture should have a mild, earthy, yeast-like aroma - if it smells putrid, discard. You will definitely know if it has gone bad, as it will have a vomit-like odor. If the mixture smells okay, use a clean spoon and taste the liquid. The flavor should be slightly tart. It may also be slightly fizzy, like a weak carbonated beverage.

After fermentation, pour the liquid from the grain jars through the cheesecloth or sprouting lid into a clean container or pitcher with a lid, loosely secure the container lid in place and refrigerate. It is important to leave the container lid slightly loose since the mixture will continue to release small amounts of carbon dioxide gas and the resulting pressure needs to escape.

Discard the grain (preferably via composting or feeding to small animals). The Rejuvelac can be stored in the refrigerator for about 2 weeks; however, fresh Rejuvelac is more potent and it will begin to lose potency the longer it is refrigerated.

During refrigeration, sediment may form at the bottom of the container - this is normal. Simply decant the liquid for use in recipes and discard the sediment at the bottom. The liquid may also begin to darken slightly after a period of time in the refrigerator. This is also normal. However, if the Rejuvelac begins to smell like vinegar, or develops a very strong sour taste, it has expired and needs to be discarded. Always test the flavor of the Rejuvelac for freshness before using in a recipe.

Buttermilk

If you've ever missed drinking a cold glass of refreshing buttermilk, then this recipe is for you. Buttermilk is also excellent for baking and for salad dressings or dip such as Buttermilk Ranch Dressing and Dip on page 27. This recipe yields 1 quart (4 cups) of the finest cultured buttermilk.

Ingredients:

- 1 cup (5 oz. by weight) whole raw cashews
- 3 cups filtered or spring water
- 1 cup Rejuvelac (pg. 23), chilled
- ½ tsp sea salt or kosher salt

You will also need a nut milk bag or a strainer lined with a double layer of cheesecloth to strain the excess solids from the buttermilk.

Technique:

Soak the nuts for a minimum of 8 hours in the refrigerator with enough filtered or spring water to cover. Drain the cashews, discarding the soaking water and place them in a high-powered blender. Add the 3 cups of fresh filtered or spring water and salt and process on high speed for 2 full minutes.

Wash your hands thoroughly and then pour the milk into the nut milk bag over a large bowl or pitcher. While holding the top of the bag with one hand, gently squeeze and knead the bag to strain the milk through the fine mesh. Discard or compost the solids in the bag. Optionally, the milk can be strained through a fine mesh strainer lined with 4 layers of cheesecloth. Use a spoon to stir the milk in the strainer to help it pass through the mesh.

Now stir in the chilled Rejuvelac. Pour into a mason jar or other similar container and cover loosely with a lid. Set aside to culture at room temperature for 24 to 36 hours (culturing will take longer at cooler temperatures and more rapidly during the warmer months). The mixture will separate while culturing - this is normal.

Smell the liquid after 24 hours - the scent of sour milk will indicate that the buttermilk is ready to be refrigerated. If the milk does not smell sour, continue to culture for an additional 12 hours.

After culturing, put the lid in place, tighten with the lid ring and shake thoroughly. Slightly loosen the lid and refrigerate (loosening the lid will allow the escape of carbon dioxide gas produced from any further fermentation). Chill for 12 hours before using and be sure to retighten the lid before shaking.

Buttermilk Ranch
Dressing and Dip

This recipe yields about 1 and ½ cup of tangy and creamy dressing or 1 and ⅓ cup dip.

Ingredients:

- ½ cup Cultured Buttermilk for dressing; or
  ⅓ cup Cultured Buttermilk for dip (see preceding recipe)
- 1 cup No-Eggy Mayo (pg. 133)
- 1 tsp onion powder
- 1 tsp Dijon mustard
- ¼ tsp garlic powder
- ¼ tsp sea salt or kosher salt, or more to taste
- ¼ tsp coarse ground black pepper, or more to taste
- ¼ tsp vegan Worcestershire sauce
- 1 T finely chopped fresh chives or 1 tsp dried
- 1 T finely chopped fresh parsley or 1 tsp dried
- 1 and ½ tsp finely chopped fresh dill or a ½ tsp dry

Technique:

In a mixing bowl, whisk all the ingredients together except for the herbs until smooth. The ingredients can also be combined in a shaker cup with a tight-fitting lid. Taste and add additional salt or pepper or thin with additional buttermilk to suit your taste. Stir in the herbs and pour into a sealable container (or store in the shaker cup). Refrigerate for a few hours to blend the flavors.

Sour Cream

Rich, tangy and velvety smooth, this recipe yields about 2 cups of the finest non-dairy sour cream - with no straining necessary. A high-powered blender is required for this recipe.

Ingredients:

- 1 and ½ cup (7.5 oz. by weight) whole raw cashews
- 2 T organic refined coconut oil
- ¾ cup Rejuvelac (pg. 23), chilled
- ¼ tsp sea salt or kosher salt

Technique:

Soak the nuts for a minimum of 8 hours in the refrigerator with enough filtered or spring water to cover. Drain the nuts, discarding the soaking water, and add them to the blender.

Remove the metal lid from the jar of coconut oil and place the jar in a microwave. Heat just until the solid oil liquefies, about 30 seconds to 1 minute (this will depend upon the solidity of the coconut oil). Alternately, you can place the jar in about an inch of simmering water and melt the oil in the same manner. Measure 2 tablespoons and add to the blender. Add the chilled Rejuvelac and the salt.

Process the contents until completely smooth, stopping to stir or scrape down the sides of blender as necessary. Avoid processing for more than 2 minutes (this can overheat the mixture through friction and potentially harm the culture).

Transfer the mixture to a clean container with a lid and cover. Let culture at room temperature for 24 to 36 hours (warmer weather will accelerate the culturing process, so taste-test after 24 hours for the proper tanginess).

The sour cream will develop an "airy" texture during culturing. This is caused by the release of carbon dioxide gas during fermentation and is perfectly normal.

After culturing, stir the sour cream thoroughly. Smooth the surface with the back of a spoon and place a layer of plastic wrap directly in contact with the sour cream. This will discourage the harmless surface discoloration that may occur during extended storage.

Seal the container and place in the refrigerator to chill for 12 hours before using. The sour cream will continue to develop flavor as it chills.

Crème Fraîche

Crème Fraîche is a cultured cream with a lower viscosity and a milder flavor than American-style sour cream. This recipe yields 2 cups.

To prepare Crème Fraîche, follow the preceding recipe for Sour Cream, but reduce the coconut oil to 1 tablespoon and culture the cream for 24 hours.

After culturing, stir the Crème Fraîche thoroughly. Seal the container and place in the refrigerator to chill for 12 hours before using. The Crème Fraîche will continue to develop flavor as it chills.

Herbs can be added prior to serving, if desired, to accommodate various ethnic cuisines (cilantro Crème Fraîche, for example, is an excellent topping for Tex-Mex Cuisine).

Tip: A quick Crème Fraîche can be prepared by diluting Sour Cream with a little non-dairy milk until the desired consistency is achieved.

Greek-Style Yogurt

This recipe produces a thick, creamy, tangy, unflavored and unsweetened yogurt that requires no additional thickening agents such as starches or gels. So why make your own yogurt? Because most commercial yogurts, even the "plain" varieties, have too much sugar added, too many thickening agents added and yet are still too runny to be useful for savory condiments such as Greek Tzatziki and Indian Raita (which require a thick, unsweetened yogurt base). Of course this yogurt can also be sweetened to your liking with organic sugar, natural syrups, fresh fruit or fruit preserves.

The yogurt is made using a blend of whole raw cashews and plain unsweetened commercial or homemade soymilk (with no additives). In my experience, this combination seems to work better than using cashew milk or soymilk alone. The micro-fine solids from the whole raw cashews add creaminess and act as a natural thickener. The cashews also contain the ideal amount of natural sugar to feed the beneficial bacterial strains, which in turn creates the yogurt.

For the best results, I recommend using a commercial yogurt maker. Yogurt makers maintain the yogurt at a specific temperature for an extended period of time and are convenient and reasonably affordable.

This recipe yields about 5 cups of yogurt. Yogurt makers will accommodate varying amounts of yogurt depending on the brand. For example, the EuroCuisine™ yogurt maker has seven jars and each jar will hold ¾ cup liquid if filled to the rim. 5 cups of yogurt will fill seven jars with a little room left at the top of each jar. The Yo'Gourmet™ yogurt maker on the other hand, has a single 2 qt. canister and is more than large enough to accommodate 5 cups of yogurt. The yogurt can also be made using a large slow-cooker (crock pot) and short, pint-size mason jars (canning jars). To do this, fold a cloth kitchen towel in half and then in half again and place on the bottom of the slow-cooker. Set the temperature to "warm".

It is important to make sure all your containers and working tools are very clean before you begin so as not to contaminate the yogurt with undesirable bacteria or molds.

Ingredients:

- 4 cups (1 quart) plain unsweetened commercial soymilk with no additives
  or 4 cups homemade Plain Unsweetened Soymilk (pg. 14)
- 1 cup (5 oz. by weight) whole raw cashews
- ½ cup commercial plain non-dairy yogurt*
  or ½ cup yogurt from the previous batch

*Commercial plain non-dairy yogurt is necessary to get the yogurt started. Non-dairy yogurt cultures are available through the internet (e.g., www.CulturesforHealth.com), but I find it much easier and less expensive to purchase a small container of plain non-dairy yogurt from the market. After that, new batches of yogurt can be started with ½ cup of yogurt from the previous batch. Commercial plain non-dairy yogurt does contain some sugar, but only a trace amount will be present after blending with the soymilk and cashews. The trace amount of sugar will then become even more dilute when making subsequent batches using yogurt from the previous batch. When purchasing non-dairy yogurt, be sure the expiration date is not too near, as fresher yogurt will contain more bacterial potency than yogurt that has been stored in market refrigerators for any length of time.

Technique:

Soak the nuts for a minimum of 8 hours in the refrigerator with enough filtered or spring water to cover. When you are ready to begin, remove the glass jars and switch on the power to warm the yogurt maker (or slow-cooker). Drain the nuts, discarding the soaking water, and place them into a high-powered blender. Add the soymilk and process on high speed for 2 full minutes.

Pour the mixture through a strainer into a large saucepan. This will eliminate any stray larger particles. Do not use a nut milk bag or cheesecloth for straining as this will strain the nut solids completely and the finer solids are necessary for thickening the yogurt. Place the saucepan over medium heat on the stove. Stir slowly but continually to prevent the milk from scorching. As the mixture heats, it will begin to thicken and foam. Just as the mixture begins to rise in the saucepan, remove the pan immediately from the heat. Set a timer for 45 minutes to let the mixture cool.

WARNING! Do not leave the saucepan unattended while the mixture is heating as it can quickly boil over.

Stir the mixture occasionally to assist even cooling and to prevent a "skin" from forming on top of the cream. After 45 minutes, feel the sides of the saucepan; it should feel comfortably warm, not hot. If it still feels hot, continue to let cool another 5 minutes or so until comfortably warm to the touch. This is important! If the mixture is too hot, it will kill the culture.

Now whisk in the yogurt starter until thoroughly combined. Pour the mixture into the yogurt jars. Do not screw the lids on the jars. Set the open jars into the yogurt maker (or slow-cooker); put the unit lid in place and culture for 6 to 8 hours. After the 6th hour, taste a spoonful of yogurt. If it is thick and has a nice tang, it is ready. If not, continue to culture for an additional hour or two.

After culturing, screw the lids on the jars and refrigerate for 12 hours. This will further develop the flavor. While refrigerating, a small amount of liquid, or whey, may collect on the sides and bottom of the jars. This is normal. Consume the yogurt within 3 weeks (because this is a cultured food, it may stay fresh longer, but 3 weeks is a rough guideline). Be sure to reserve ½ cup for starting your next batch.

Tzatziki

Tzatziki is a Greek cucumber sauce used as a condiment for Greek and other Mediterranean cuisine and is traditionally made with thick plain dairy yogurt. Commercial non-dairy plain yogurt would seem the obvious alternate to dairy yogurt, but even the plain varieties contain substantial amounts of sugar and are too sweet (and too runny) for this dish. Homemade Greek-style yogurt works best. This recipe yields about 2 cups of sauce.

Ingredients:

- 1 small cucumber, peeled or unpeeled, seeded and diced
- 1 cup Greek-Style Yogurt (pg. 30)
- 2 T olive oil
- ¼ cup finely minced red onion
- 2 cloves garlic, finely minced
- 2 tsp red wine vinegar or raw apple cider vinegar
- ¼ tsp sea salt or kosher salt, or more to taste
- ¼ tsp coarse ground black pepper, or more to taste
- 1 tsp chopped fresh dill (optional)

Technique:

Wrap the diced cucumber in a few layers of paper towels or a lint-free kitchen towel and squeeze to remove the excess moisture. Add the cucumbers and the remaining ingredients to the yogurt and stir until well combined. Taste the mixture and add a little more salt or pepper, as desired. Chill for at least two hours to blend the flavors. If you like, garnish with a sprig of fresh dill just before serving.

Indian Raita

Raita is an Indian, Pakistani and Bangladeshi condiment traditionally made with thick dairy yogurt (dahi), cucumber and seasonings and used as a sauce or dip to temper the heat of Indian spices. Commercial non-dairy plain yogurt would seem the obvious alternate to dairy yogurt, but even the plain varieties contain substantial amounts of sugar and are too sweet (and too runny) for this dish. Homemade Greek-style yogurt works best. This recipe yields about 2 cups of sauce.

Ingredients:

- 1 small cucumber, peeled or unpeeled, seeded and diced
- 1 and ½ cup Greek-Style Yogurt (pg. 30)
- 2 T olive oil
- ¼ cup finely chopped scallions (green onions) including green tops
- 2 tsp fresh lemon juice
- ½ tsp sea salt or kosher salt, or more to taste
- ¼ tsp ground cumin
- 2 T chopped fresh mint (optional)

Technique:

Wrap the diced cucumber in a few layers of paper towels or a lint-free kitchen towel and squeeze to remove the excess moisture. Add the cucumber and the remaining ingredients to the yogurt and stir until well combined. Taste the mixture and add a little more lemon juice, salt or cumin, as desired. Chill for at least two hours to blend the flavors. If you like, garnish with a sprig of fresh mint just before serving.

An Introduction to Non-Dairy Cheeses

While commercial non-dairy cheeses have made vast improvements since they were first marketed many years ago, I feel that most of them still lack something in flavor and/or texture. Since the publication of my first cookbook, I have spent many months researching the properties of dairy cheese and experimenting with various plant-based ingredients to create cheeses that simulate their dairy counterparts as closely as possible.

Dairy cheese is comprised of proteins and fat from milk, usually the milk of cows, buffalo, goats, or sheep. It is produced by coagulation of the milk protein casein. Typically, the milk is acidified and the addition of the enzyme rennet (derived from the stomachs of cows, goats and sheep) causes coagulation. The solids are then separated and pressed into final form. For a few cheeses, such as mascarpone and paneer, the milk is curdled by adding acids such as vinegar or lemon juice.

Most dairy cheeses are acidified by bacteria, which turns milk sugar (lactose) into lactic acid, with the addition of rennet completing the curdling process. At this stage, the cheese is considered fresh or unripened. Varieties that fall into this category include cottage cheese, cream cheese and ricotta.

Other varieties are ripened by the addition of various strains of bacteria and molds and then aged for varying periods of time. Ripened cheeses are further classified by texture or process.

However, non-dairy cheeses need to be produced using completely different processes since plant milks do not contain casein and since rennet is not used (and would not be used for ethical reasons) as a coagulant. Vegetarian rennet does exist (enzymes derived from various microbial and plant sources), but it only works with animal milk.

In this book, a culturing process, an uncultured cooking process and an uncultured "cold" blending process* are used to produce non-dairy cheeses according to different criteria: melting ability; textures ranging from soft and spreadable to firm and solid; and/or varying degrees of sharpness.

* The tofu-based cheeses are "cold-blended" cheeses; in other words there is no cooking involved other than the warming required to melt the coconut oil for measuring.

Sharpness is best described as a complex, acidic and tangy flavor. It is important to note, however, that not all ripened cheeses are sharp. Gouda and Gruyère, for example, have very rich, developed flavors which cannot be described exactly as "sharp" or acidic.

Cheddars and blues are the most common cheeses described as sharp, although others are sometimes grouped this way as well. While the method of production dictates a cheese's sharpness, ultimately it is simply a measure used to categorize the flavor of the cheese.

The degree of sharpness in dairy cheddar cheese, for example, is determined by the breakdown of fats and proteins by bacteria and enzymes during aging. In other words, the longer the cheddar ages, the sharper it gets (9 months minimum for sharp cheddars and 15 months minimum for extra-sharp). This process produces compounds (*aldehydes* and *alpha-keto acids*) and other flavors (*esters*) that give the cheddar a sharp or tangy taste.

For the cultured cashew-based cheeses in this book, truly sharp flavors are produced by brief periods of bacterial fermentation and ripening (brief when compared to dairy cheeses).

For the uncultured cheeses, such as the soymilk and tofu-based cheeses, mild to moderate degrees of sharpness and ripened flavor qualities are simulated by using blends of fruit acids and other natural ingredients. These combinations mimic flavors which would normally be produced by bacterial culturing and ripening. Both processes are much less complicated than dairy cheese production and more instantly gratifying (although a little more patience is required for the cultured cheeses).

For questions and advice regarding the recipes,
please join the Gentle Chef Group on Facebook:
https://www.facebook.com/groups/thegentlechef

To view the full-color photo gallery of the recipes in this book,
please visit The Gentle Chef website at: http://thegentlechef.com

Cultured Cashew-Based Cheeses

As stated previously, the cultured cashew-based cheeses derive their tangy flavor, or sharpness, from actual culturing (fermentation) with "friendly" bacteria, rather than through the use of fruit acids such as vinegar and lemon juice. A thick emulsion of raw cashews is used as the medium for culturing and Rejuvelac is used as the culturing agent.

A cashew emulsion is prepared by grinding raw cashews that have been soaked in water until hydrated. This creates an entirely different composition than cashew butter which is prepared by grinding raw or roasted cashews.

The degree of sharpness is determined by the period of time the cheese is cultured at room temperature, usually from 1 to 3 days, depending on the cheese and the ambient temperature. During this time, the lactobacillus bacteria convert the natural sugars in the cashew emulsion into lactic acid, which provides the tangy flavor. In some cases, mellow white miso paste is added as a secondary culturing agent, which enhances the flavor of the cheese as it cultures and then ripens. Other natural ingredients may be included for imparting unique and complex flavor characteristics to the cheese.

Because the cheeses contain live cultures, seaweed derivatives such as carrageenan and agar are not used as gelling agents, since both require heat for activation. Instead, refined coconut oil is used as a thickener, which depending on the amount specified in the recipe, will create textures ranging from soft and spreadable to semi-firm and crumbly. The coconut oil also provides the fat necessary to produce the proper "melt-in-your-mouth" quality to the cheeses. However, while the cultured cheeses will soften when exposed to heat, they will not melt in the same manner as the soymilk-based block cheeses and they definitely will not stretch.

A food processor and a high-powered blender are required for efficient processing. Since processing foods in a high-powered blender can generate a great deal of heat through friction, the food processor is used first to break the cashews down into a coarse paste. By initially breaking down the cashews into a coarse paste, the running time on the blender is then reduced, which ensures that the bacterial culture is not destroyed by excessive exposure to heat. The high-powered blender is essential as it processes the cashews into the smoothest texture possible, which is something the food processor cannot do alone. DO NOT attempt to use a standard blender for these recipes, as you will quickly burn out the motor!

The cultured cheeses are produced in somewhat larger portions (about 12 oz.) than you might normally purchase of their dairy counterparts (typically 4 to 8 oz.). This is because a larger volume of material is easier to process in the blender and inevitably the small amount of product that cannot be retrieved from under the blender blades will be lost. However, since the cheeses are cultured, they can be refrigerated for several weeks and you won't have to prepare them as often.

Cream Cheese

This recipe produces the finest, cultured non-dairy cream cheese. A food processor and a high-powered blender are required for efficient processing. This recipe yields about 12 oz.

Ingredients:

- 1 and ½ cups (7.5 oz. by weight) whole raw cashews
- ¼ cup organic refined coconut oil
- ½ tsp sea salt or kosher salt
- ⅓ cup Rejuvelac (pg. 23), chilled

Technique:

Soak the nuts for a minimum of 8 hours in the refrigerator with enough filtered or spring water to cover. Drain the nuts, discarding the soaking water, and add them to a food processor.

Remove the metal lid from the jar of coconut oil and place the jar in a microwave. Heat just until the solid oil liquefies, about 30 seconds to 1 minute (this will depend upon the solidity of the coconut oil). Alternately, you can place the jar in about an inch of simmering water and melt the oil in the same manner. Measure ¼ cup and add to the food processor with the salt. Process the cashews into a coarse paste, about 2 minutes.

Transfer the cashew paste to the blender; add the chilled Rejuvelac and process on high speed until completely smooth. The mixture will be very thick, so stop to scrape down the sides of the blender and push the mixture down into the blades as necessary. Use a tamper tool if provided with your blender to keep the mixture turning in the blades. Avoid continual processing for more than 2 minutes, as this can overheat the mixture through friction and potentially harm the culture.

Transfer the mixture to a clean container with a lid. Cover and let the cheese culture at room temperature for 24 hours. The cream cheese may develop an "airy" texture during culturing. This is caused by the release of carbon dioxide gas during fermentation and is perfectly normal.

After culturing, stir the cream cheese thoroughly. Smooth the surface with the back of a spoon and place a layer of plastic wrap directly in contact with the cheese. This will discourage the harmless surface discoloration that may occur during extended storage. Now seal the container and place in the refrigerator to chill for 12 hours before using. The cream cheese will continue to develop flavor as it chills.

Variations: For cream cheese with onion and chives, stir in 1 T dried minced onion and 1 T freeze-dried minced chives **before** chilling. For fruit flavored cream cheese, mix ¼ cup all-fruit jam into the cream cheese **after** it has chilled and firmed.

Cream Cheese Jack-Crab Rangoon

Rangoon are deep-fried dumplings stuffed with a combination of cream cheese, flaked imitation crab meat (made from green jackfruit), green onion and other seasonings. The filling is enclosed in wonton wrappers in a triangular or flower-shape and then deep fried in vegetable oil.

Canned green jackfruit is used in this recipe to simulate the texture of crab meat. It has no real flavor of its own and no protein value, but it has an uncanny resemblance to crab meat when shredded.

Canned green jackfruit can be found in Indian and Asian markets. Look for the label "Green Jackfruit" or "Young Green Jackfruit" and be sure that it's packed in water or brine, not syrup. You may notice cans of ripe jackfruit stocked nearby but don't be tempted to substitute as it is very sweet when ripe and often packed in sugar syrup.

Rangoon Ingredients:

- 8 oz. (1 cup) Cream Cheese (pg. 37)
- 1 can (20 oz.) green jackfruit in water or brine
- 2 T water chestnuts, finely chopped (optional)
- 1 green onion including the green top, finely chopped
- 1 tsp tamari, soy sauce or Bragg Liquid Aminos™
- 1 tsp finely minced garlic (1 clove)
- ¼ tsp ground white pepper
- Wonton Wrappers (recipe included)
- vegetable oil for deep-frying

Wonton Wrapper Ingredients:

- 1 and ⅓ cup rice flour
- ⅔ cup all-purpose flour
- ⅞ cup hot water (¾ cup plus 2 T)
- 2 tsp sea salt or kosher salt
- additional all-purpose flour for rolling

Technique:

Drain the liquid from the can of jackfruit and rinse the fruit thoroughly (especially if it was packed in brine) and drain in a colander. With a sharp knife, remove the tough core from each chunk of jackfruit and discard. Break the chunks apart with your fingers and remove the soft seeds and discard.

Cook the jackfruit in simmering water for 10 minutes. Drain and set aside to cool. Once cooled, wrap the pulp in a layer of paper towels or a lint-free kitchen towel and squeeze to remove as much water as possible.

Place the jackfruit into a food processor and pulse to shred into flakes. Do not purée. Place the flakes in a mixing bowl and add the remaining Rangoon ingredients (reserve half of the green onion to garnish the tops). Stir thoroughly to combine, cover and place in the refrigerator until ready to assemble the Rangoon.

For the wonton wrappers, stir the flours, hot water and salt in a mixing bowl with a sturdy spoon until a sticky ball of dough forms. Cover the ball of dough with a damp towel and let rest for 10 minutes.

Now, flour a work surface with all-purpose flour and transfer the dough to the work surface. Sprinkle the dough with a little all-purpose flour and knead until smooth. Repeat as necessary until the dough is no longer sticky.

Next, flour a rolling pin and roll out the dough as thinly as possible without tearing. Using a round object with an approximate 3" diameter (such as a ring mold, cookie cutter or drinking glass) cut out round discs of dough. Place a small amount of filling in the center of a disc. Fold the disc over (like a taco shell) and pinch the dough closed at the top. Gather in the 2 sides and pinch closed at the seams to form a little bundle. Make sure the seams are completely pinched closed. Form any remnants of dough into a ball and roll out and cut as previously described. Repeat until the filling and dough is used up.

Heat the vegetable oil in a deep fryer until the oil begins to shimmer. Drop the bundles in the hot oil and fry until golden. Remove with a slotted spoon to a paper-towel lined plate.

Serve immediately with sweet and sour sauce or hot Chinese mustard as a side condiment.

Chèvre

Ingredients:

- 1 and ½ cup (7.5 oz. by weight) whole raw cashews
- ¼ cup organic refined coconut oil
- ¾ tsp sea salt or kosher salt
- ½ tsp onion powder
- ¼ cup Rejuvelac (pg. 23), chilled

Technique:

Chèvre (from the French word for goat), is a semi-soft cheese traditionally made from the milk of goats. Non-dairy chèvre is a cultured cashew-based cheese. It has a tangy, tart and refreshing flavor. It also serves as a wonderful cheese base for adding various herbs and spices to create unique variations of flavor. A food processor and a high-powered blender are required for efficient processing. This recipe yields about 12 oz.

Soak the nuts for a minimum of 8 hours in the refrigerator with enough filtered or spring water to cover. Drain the nuts, discarding the water, and add them to a food processor.

Remove the metal lid from the jar of coconut oil and place the jar in a microwave. Heat just until the solid oil liquefies, about 30 seconds to 1 minute (this will depend upon the solidity of the coconut oil). Alternately, you can place the jar in about an inch of simmering water and melt the oil in the same manner. Measure ¼ cup and add to the food processor with the salt. Process the cashews into a coarse paste, about 2 minutes.

Transfer the cashew paste to the blender; add the chilled Rejuvelac and process on high speed until completely smooth. The mixture will be very thick, so stop to scrape down the sides of the blender and push the mixture down into the blades as necessary. Use a tamper tool if provided with your blender to keep the mixture turning in the blades. Avoid continual processing for more than 2 minutes, as this can overheat the mixture through friction and potentially harm the culture.

Transfer the mixture to a clean container with a lid. Cover and let the cheese culture at room temperature for 36 to 48 hours (warmer weather will accelerate the culturing process, so taste-test after 36 hours). The cheese will develop an "airy" texture during culturing. This is caused by the release of carbon dioxide gas during fermentation and is perfectly normal.

After culturing, stir the cheese mixture until creamy, cover and place the container in the refrigerator to chill for 12 hours until the cheese is firm.

After the cheese has chilled and firmed, lay out a sheet of plastic wrap or wax paper on your work surface. Scoop up the cheese mixture from the container and with your hands, form the mixture into a log shape. Don't worry about perfection; the plastic wrap or wax paper will shape the log when rolled. Place the log on the sheet of wrap or paper and roll the mixture like a tootsie-roll. Twist the ends tightly and place back in the refrigerator for an additional 12 hours to firm and ripen. To serve, simply remove the wrapper and place on a serving plate.

Peppercorn Chèvre

For this variation, the cultured chèvre is rolled in 1 tablespoon of crushed or cracked black peppercorns or a rainbow blend of mixed peppercorns.

First, prepare the chèvre and culture and refrigerate to firm as instructed on page 40. After firming the cheese, lay out a sheet of plastic wrap or wax paper on your work surface. Sprinkle the wrap or paper with half of the pepper. Scoop up the cheese mixture from the container and with your hands, form the mixture into a log shape. Don't worry about perfection; the plastic wrap or wax paper will shape the log when rolled.

Place the log on top of the pepper sprinkled on the sheet of wrap or paper. Sprinkle the remaining pepper on top and press into the cheese with your fingers.

Now roll the mixture inside the wrap or paper like a tootsie-roll. Twist the ends tightly and place back in the refrigerator for an additional 12 hours to firm and ripen. To serve, simply remove the wrapper and place on a serving plate.

Chèvre with Fines Herbes

In the culinary arts, the term Fines Herbes refers to a blend of herbs traditionally used in French cooking. For this variation, the cultured cheese is rolled in 1 tablespoon each of minced fresh parsley, chives, tarragon and chervil or marjoram (substitute with 1 tsp dried chervil or marjoram if you cannot obtain fresh).

First, prepare the chèvre and culture and refrigerate to firm as instructed on page 40. After firming the cheese, lay out a sheet of plastic wrap or wax paper on your work surface. Sprinkle the wrap or paper with half of the dried herbs. Scoop up the cheese mixture from the container and with your hands, form the mixture into a log shape. Don't worry about perfection; the plastic wrap or wax paper will shape the log when rolled.

Place the log on top of the herbs sprinkled on the sheet of wrap or paper. Sprinkle the remaining herbs on top and press into the cheese with your fingers. Now roll the mixture inside the wrap or paper like a tootsie-roll. Twist the ends tightly and place back in the refrigerator for an additional 12 hours to firm and ripen. To serve, simply remove the wrapper and place on a serving plate.

Chèvre with Rosemary Balsamic Swirl

For this variation, you will need 1 tablespoon of rosemary balsamic reduction (recipe below) for folding into the cheese after culturing.

First, prepare the chèvre and culture and refrigerate to firm as instructed on page 40. After firming the cheese, lay out a sheet of plastic wrap or wax paper on your work surface.

Drizzle the balsamic reduction over the cheese in the container. Fold the flavoring into the cheese with a sturdy wooden spoon - don't stir. Scoop up the cheese mixture and with your hands form the mixture into a log shape. Don't worry about perfection; the plastic wrap or wax paper will shape the log when rolled. Place the log on the sheet of wrap or paper and roll the mixture like a tootsie-roll. Twist the ends tightly and place back in the refrigerator for several hours to re-firm. To serve, simply remove the wrapper and place on a serving plate.

For the rosemary balsamic reduction, you will need:

- ½ cup dark balsamic vinegar
- 1 T organic sugar
- ½ tsp fresh minced rosemary

Technique:

In a small saucepan, stir together the vinegar, sugar and rosemary over medium heat. Cook until syrupy, about 5 minutes. Strain and use 1 tablespoon for flavoring the Chèvre. Any leftover reduction (also known as a *gastrique*) can be used for drizzling over garden salads or fresh fruit (it's especially good when drizzled over cubed watermelon).

White Cheddar Amandine

White Cheddar Amandine is semi-soft, almond-encrusted cheese log with a sharp cheddar flavor that continues to develop and intensify as it ages. A food processor and a high-powered blender are required for efficient processing. This recipe yields about 12 oz.

Ingredients:

- 1 and ½ cups (7.5 oz. by weight) whole raw cashews
- ⅓ cup organic refined coconut oil
- 2 T nutritional yeast
- 2 T mellow white miso paste
- 1 tsp onion powder
- ½ tsp sea salt or kosher salt
- ½ tsp dry ground mustard
- ¼ cup Rejuvelac (pg. 23), chilled

For the crust, you will need:

- ⅓ cup slivered raw almonds

Technique:

Soak the nuts for a minimum of 8 hours in the refrigerator with enough filtered or spring water to cover. Drain the nuts, discarding the soaking water, and add them to a food processor.

Remove the metal lid from the jar of coconut oil and place the jar in a microwave. Heat just until the solid oil liquefies, about 30 seconds to 1 minute (this will depend upon the solidity of the coconut oil). Alternately, you can place the jar in about an inch of simmering water and melt the oil in the same manner. Measure ⅓ cup and add to the food processor with the nutritional yeast, miso, onion powder and mustard powder. Process the cashews into a coarse paste, about 2 minutes.

Transfer the paste to the blender and add the chilled Rejuvelac. Process the contents on high speed until completely smooth. The mixture will be very thick, so stop to scrape down the sides of the blender and push the mixture down into the blades as necessary. Use a tamper tool if provided with your blender to keep the mixture turning in the blades. Avoid continual processing for more than 2 minutes, as this can overheat the mixture through friction and potentially harm the culture.

Transfer the mixture to a clean container with a lid. Cover and let the cheese culture at room temperature for 36 to 48 hours (warmer weather will accelerate the culturing process, so taste-test after 36 hours for the proper sharpness). The cheese will develop an "airy" texture during culturing. This is caused by the release of carbon dioxide gas during fermentation and is perfectly normal.

After culturing, stir the cheese mixture until creamy, cover and place the container in the refrigerator to chill for 12 hours until the cheese is firm.

After the cheese has chilled and firmed, place the slivered almonds into a food processor and pulse until coarsely ground. Add the ground almonds to a skillet and place over medium heat. Stir frequently until the almonds are toasted and are emitting a very nutty aroma. Be careful not let them burn! Scatter the ground toasted almonds on a plate and allow them to cool before proceeding.

Lay out a sheet of plastic wrap or wax paper on your work surface and set aside.

Next, scoop up the cheese mixture and with your hands and form the mixture into a log shape. Don't worry about perfection; the wrap will shape the log when rolled. Roll the log in the ground nuts on the plate, gently pressing the nuts into the cheese with your fingers.

Place the log on the wrap and roll the cheese like a tootsie-roll inside the wrap; twist the ends tightly. Place back in the refrigerator for 48 hours to continue to ripen. To serve, simply remove the wrap, place on a serving plate and slice as needed.

Crumbly Extra-Sharp White Cheddar

Crumbly Extra-Sharp White Cheddar is a semi-firm snacking cheese with a crumbly texture and extra-sharp cheddar flavor that continues to develop and intensify as it ages. It's sure to please the most discerning sharp cheddar connoisseur. A food processor and a high-powered blender are required for efficient processing. This recipe yields about 12 oz.

Ingredients:

- 1 and ½ cups (7.5 oz. by weight) whole raw cashews
- ½ cup organic refined coconut oil
- 2 T nutritional yeast
- 2 T mellow white miso paste
- 1 tsp onion powder
- ½ tsp sea salt or kosher salt
- ½ tsp dry ground mustard
- ¼ cup Rejuvelac (pg. 23), chilled

Technique:

Soak the nuts for a minimum of 8 hours in the refrigerator with enough filtered or spring water to cover. Drain the nuts, discarding the soaking water, and add them to a food processor.

Remove the metal lid from the jar of coconut oil and place the jar in a microwave. Heat just until the solid oil liquefies, about 30 seconds to 1 minute (this will depend upon the solidity of the coconut oil). Alternately, you can place the jar in about an inch of simmering water and melt the oil in the same manner. Measure ½ cup and add to the food processor with the nutritional yeast, miso, onion powder and mustard powder. Process the cashews into a coarse paste, about 2 minutes.

Transfer the paste to the blender and add the chilled Rejuvelac. Process the contents on high speed until completely smooth. The mixture will be very thick, so stop to scrape down the sides of the blender and push the mixture down into the blades as necessary. Use a tamper tool if provided with your blender to keep the mixture turning in the blades. Avoid continual processing for more than 2 minutes, as this can overheat the mixture through friction and potentially harm the culture.

Transfer the mixture to a clean container with a lid, cover and let the cheese culture at room temperature for 48 to 72 hours (warmer weather will accelerate the culturing process, so taste-test after 48 hours for the proper sharpness). The cheese will develop an "airy" texture during culturing. This is caused by the release of carbon dioxide gas during fermentation and is perfectly normal.

After culturing, line a round, square or rectangular container that will hold a minimum of 2 cups liquid with plastic wrap. Be sure to leave excess wrap hanging over the sides. The container will serve as a form to shape the cheese and the plastic wrap will help lift the cheese from the container after firming.

Stir the cheese until creamy and then transfer to the prepared form. Press the cheese mixture thoroughly into the form and smooth the surface with the back of a spoon as best you can. Cover and place the container in the refrigerator for 72 hours to firm and ripen.

To serve, simply lift the cheese from the form, remove the plastic wrap and slice as needed. Keep the cheese stored in the refrigerator wrapped tightly in plastic or in a zip-lock bag. The cheese will continue to develop flavor and become more crumbly as it ages.

Bleu Cheese

Dairy blue cheese has a very distinct, pungent aroma and flavor created by the mold Penicillium roqueforti, as well as by specially cultivated bacteria. This mold is also responsible for the blue-green "veins" within the cheese.

Admittedly, mimicking the flavor and appearance of blue cheese with plant-based ingredients available to the home vegan cook was a bit of a challenge. Although it lacks some of the pungency of dairy blue cheese normally created by the Penicillium mold, it has a sharp, tangy flavor, a semi-firm crumbly texture and the characteristic blue-green "veins" that give bleu cheese its name. A food processor and a high-powered blender are required for efficient processing. This recipe yields about 12 oz.

Ingredients:

- 1 and ½ cup (7.5 oz. by weight) whole raw cashews
- ½ cup organic refined coconut oil
- 1 T mellow white miso paste
- 1 and ¼ tsp sea salt or kosher salt
- 1 tsp onion powder
- ½ tsp garlic powder
- ¼ cup Rejuvelac (pg. 23), chilled
- ¼ tsp blue-green algae powder (spirulina)

Technique:

Soak the nuts for a minimum of 8 hours in the refrigerator with enough filtered or spring water to cover. Drain the nuts, discarding the soaking water and add them to a food processor.

Remove the metal lid from the jar of coconut oil and place the jar in a microwave. Heat just until the solid oil liquefies, about 30 seconds to 1 minute (this will depend upon the solidity of the coconut oil). Alternately, you can place the jar in about an inch of simmering water and melt the oil in the same manner. Measure ½ cup and add to the food processor. Process the cashews into a coarse paste, about 2 minutes.

Transfer the cashew paste to the blender; add the miso, salt, onion powder, garlic powder and chilled Rejuvelac and process until completely smooth. The mixture will be very thick, so stop to scrape down the sides of the blender and push the mixture down into the blades as necessary. Use a tamper tool if provided with your blender to keep the mixture turning in the blades. Avoid continual processing for more than 2 minutes, as this can overheat the mixture through friction and potentially harm the culture.

Transfer the mixture to a clean container with a lid, cover and let the cheese culture at room temperature for 48 to 72 hours (warmer weather will accelerate the culturing process, so taste-test after 48 hours for the proper sharpness). The cheese will develop an "airy" texture during culturing. This is caused by the release of carbon dioxide gas during fermentation and is perfectly normal.

After culturing, remove the lid and stir the cheese until creamy and then dot the surface of the cheese in several places with the algae powder. Now fold (rather than stir) the cheese over a few times to create swirls of blue-green color. Scoop the cheese into another clean container lined with plastic wrap. The plastic wrap will help lift the cheese from the form after chilling and ripening. Pack the cheese into the container and smooth the surface with the back of a spoon. Cover with a lid or plastic wrap and refrigerate for 72 hours.

After 72 hours, lift the cheese from the form and remove the plastic wrap. The cheese is now ready to slice or crumble as needed. Store tightly wrapped in plastic wrap or a zip-lock bag. The cheese will become firmer, more crumbly and the flavor will continue to develop as the cheese ages. Do not freeze.

Chunky Bleu Cheese Dressing

This incredible non-dairy dressing tastes remarkably like restaurant-style dairy blue cheese dressing. This dressing is also excellent when served as a dip for crudités (assorted sliced raw vegetables).

Ingredients:

- 4 oz. Bleu Cheese (pg. 47)
- 1 cup No-Eggy Mayo (pg. 133)
- 3 T Sour Cream (pg. 28)
- 2 T non-dairy milk, or more to adjust consistency
- ¼ tsp coarse ground black pepper, or more to taste
- ¼ tsp sea salt or kosher salt, or more to taste
- ¼ tsp vegan Worcestershire sauce

Technique:

Add ½ of the crumbled bleu cheese and the remaining ingredients to a food processor and process the contents until smooth, about 30 seconds. If you wish to thin the consistency, add more non-dairy milk a tablespoon at a time until the desired consistency is achieved; season with additional salt and pepper to taste. Transfer to a covered container and stir in the remaining crumbled bleu cheese. Seal the container and refrigerate until well-chilled before using.

Soymilk-Based Block Cheeses

I had several goals in mind when I began working on the recipes in this book and one of my greatest challenges was to produce cheeses that behave just like their dairy counterparts in terms of slicing, shredding and/or melting ability. After experimenting extensively with various plant ingredients in different combinations and ratios, I was finally successful at producing cheeses that satisfied my criteria.

Plain unsweetened soymilk is required for these cheeses. Soymilk is a stable emulsion (meaning it does not separate) and is the closest to dairy milk in terms of composition. This stability and composition enables it to emulsify with refined coconut oil, which in turn creates the cheese (emulsification refers to the process of binding fat molecules and water molecules together). It has been my experience that other plant milks will not emulsify with the coconut oil properly. Regrettably for those allergic or sensitive to soy, there is no substitute for the soymilk.

For the cheeses in this section, as well as for cheese sauces, melts and fondue, it is essential to use soymilk that is free of gums, starches, gels (such as carrageenan) and sweeteners, as these additives will adversely affect the flavor, cooking process and finished texture of the cheese. This is logical since tapioca flour, a starch, is already specified in all of the soymilk-based recipes in this book and kappa carrageenan is already included in the cheese recipes in this section. However, vitamin and calcium fortified soymilk is acceptable and will not affect results.

Westsoy™ produces an unsweetened, organic, non-GMO and additive-free soymilk which is ideal for the block cheese recipes (as well as for cheese sauces, melts and fondue). Homemade soymilk is the next best option if commercial additive-free soymilk is unavailable. However, homemade soymilk must be thoroughly strained to remove as much of the okara (pulp) as possible; if not, the cheese will have a pasty texture when melted. Detailed instructions are provided with the recipe for Plain Unsweetened Soymilk on page 14.

Refined coconut oil provides the necessary fat which transforms the blended and cooked ingredients into cheese. Without the fat, the mixture would simply be a gelled block of flavored soymilk. The coconut oil also contributes to the firmness of the cheese, since it solidifies when chilled, and enables the cheese to melt evenly when exposed to heat. Avoid virgin coconut oil for cheese making, as it will impart an undesirable coconut flavor. Refined coconut oil can only be substituted with organic de-scented cocoa butter, which can be expensive and often difficult to find.

Tapioca flour, or starch, is used as a thickening agent. It also provides "stretch" when the cheeses are melted. Other starches will not work in the same manner, so there is no exact substitute.

Depending on the variety of cheese, nutritional yeast is sometimes included because of its cheesy flavor and golden color. Fruit acids are used in small amounts to simulate the flavor of lactic acid, a by-product which occurs in traditionally cultured and ripened cheeses. Sea salt or kosher salt is used as a common flavoring and other seasonings may be specified to add unique flavor qualities.

Carrageenan, a derivative of seaweed, is used as a firming agent because of its heat-reversible properties. "Heat-reversible" refers to it ability to re-melt when exposed to heat after it has already been set (unlike agar, which is not heat-reversible). Agar cannot be used as a substitute for carrageenan in these recipes.

A form will be needed for shaping and firming the block of cheese, except for Fresh Mozzarella, which is scooped into round balls and firmed in a chilled brine. Any glass or ceramic bowl or BPA-free plastic container that will hold a minimum of 2 cups liquid will work. Consider the variety of cheese when choosing the shape of the container. For example, Camembert and Brie are traditionally shaped in a round "wheel", whereas cheddars can be shaped in round, square or rectangular blocks.

The ingredients will need to be processed in a blender before cooking. A high-powered blender is not required. The ingredients should be processed on a low speed just until blended and smooth. Over-processing at high speed is not necessary and will cause the mixture to become excessively thick and difficult to pour from the blender. If you think about it, high speed blending with soymilk and oil makes mayonnaise. It's the same principle here. Also, allow the soymilk to reach room temperature before blending, since chilled soymilk has a tendency to harden the melted coconut oil in the blender, thus creating an excessively thick and grainy mixture which is more difficult to pour from the blender.

Once blended, the mixture is cooked over medium-low heat while continually stirred with a flexible rubber or silicone spatula. As the mixture heats, it will begin to form lumps, or "curds". As this occurs, the stirring speed is increased until the mixture becomes a very smooth and glossy mass of melted cheese. If non-stick cookware is used, the cheese will often pull away from the sides of the pan. Once the mixture appears smooth and has an obvious glossy sheen, it's ready and should be removed from the heat. The entire cooking process should not take more than 5 to 6 minutes, sometimes less.

Once cooked, the melted cheese is immediately and quickly transferred to the form before it begins to set. Attempting to smooth the surface at this point is futile, as the cheese will be very sticky, so it should be allowed to settle on its own for a few minutes. After settling and setting for a few minutes, the surface can be smoothed with the spatula if desired; however, a smooth surface isn't really essential, since the surface will become the bottom of the cheese once removed from its form.

The cheese is then left to cool until it nears room temperature. Once cooled, the form is covered with plastic wrap, with the wrap coming into contact with the surface of the cheese, and refrigerated for a minimum of 6 hours to firm completely before being removed from the form.

After the cheese has been chilled and firmed completely, it is removed from its form. Blotting with a paper towel is recommended to remove moisture that has precipitated to the exterior of the cheese. This precipitation is caused by the tapioca starch used in preparation. Anytime a mixture is cooked with starch (tapioca starch, cornstarch, potato starch, etc.) and then refrigerated, moisture will precipitate from the mixture. This precipitation also occurs with puddings, pie fillings and cheesecakes prepared with starch as a thickener.

The cheese is now ready to be sliced or shredded as needed. It is also recommended that the cheese be wrapped in a paper towel (except for Brie and Camembert) before being sealed in plastic wrap or a zip-lock bag and stored in the refrigerator. The paper towel will continue to absorb any further precipitation, which contributes to a drier, firmer texture. The paper towel should be replaced every few days.

Please note that the block cheeses need an evenly hot temperature to melt properly (which is also true of most dairy cheeses). For example, if you place a slice of block cheese on a cold sandwich and then place it under a broiler, the cold temperature of the sandwich will inhibit melting. The cheese will eventually melt, but it will take some coaxing and you could potentially burn the bread of the sandwich. Try finely shredding the cheese, as it will melt quicker than sliced cheese; or better yet, heat the sandwich filling before adding the cheese.

For foods that would otherwise burn before the cheese is melted, such as grilled cheese sandwiches, try one of the Cheese Melts (pg. 103). For foods that cool quickly, such as nachos or cheesy fries, the Cheese Sauces (pg. 92) are the best option.

Americana

Americana is a firm, mild cheese with a classic American cheese flavor. Thin slices are superb for cold sandwiches or for melting on burgers or other grilled sandwiches. This cheese can also be finely shredded and used in your favorite recipes.

For this recipe you will need a glass, ceramic or BPA-free plastic container which will hold a minimum of 2 cups liquid; this will act as the form to shape the cheese.

Ingredients:

- 1 and ⅓ cup plain unsweetened soymilk with no additives (see pg. 8)
- ½ cup organic refined coconut oil
- ¼ cup tapioca flour
- ¼ cup nutritional yeast
- 4 tsp kappa carrageenan
- 1 T mellow white miso paste
- 2 tsp organic tomato paste
- 1 tsp dry ground mustard
- 1 tsp sea salt or kosher salt
- ½ tsp onion powder

Technique:

Measure the soymilk and let it come to room temperature (if chilled).

Remove the lid from the jar of coconut oil and place the jar in a microwave. Heat until the solid oil liquefies, about 30 seconds to 1 minute (this will depend upon the solidity of the coconut oil). Alternately, you can place the jar in about an inch of simmering water and melt the oil in the same manner. Measure ½ cup and pour into a blender.

Add the soymilk and the remaining ingredients to the blender and process on low speed until smooth, stopping to scrape down the sides of the blender as necessary with a rubber/silicone spatula.

Transfer the mixture to a saucepan and cook over medium-low heat, slowly and continuously stirring with a flexible rubber/silicone spatula and scraping the sides and bottom of the saucepan as necessary. Increase stirring speed as the mixture thickens and begins to form curds. Stir vigorously until the mixture becomes very thick, smooth and glossy (if using non-stick cookware, the cheese should pull away from the sides of the pan).

Now quickly transfer the melted cheese to the container but do not attempt to smooth the surface (the cheese will be too sticky); let the cheese settle on its own, or rap the container sharply on your work surface to help the cheese settle. Let the cheese cool at room temperature for about 20 minutes. Cover with plastic wrap, making sure the wrap comes into contact with the surface of the cheese and refrigerate for a minimum of 6 hours or until completely chilled and very firm.

When the cheese has been completely chilled and firmed, invert the container and tap sharply to remove (if necessary, carefully run a table knife around the inside perimeter to loosen). Wrap the cheese snugly in a paper towel and then wrap tightly in plastic wrap or seal in a zip-lock bag. Refrigerate for 24 hours. The paper towel will absorb any moisture released from the cheese during refrigeration and contribute to a firmer, drier texture.

Remove the paper towel and slice or shred as needed. Store the cheese in the refrigerator wrapped in a dry paper towel and then plastic wrap or a zip-lock bag (squeeze out as much air as possible before sealing). Replace the paper towel every few days.

English Cheddar

English Cheddar is a firm cheese with a golden color and tangy flavor. Thin slices are ideal for cold sandwiches or for melting on burgers or other grilled sandwiches. English cheddar can also be finely shredded and used in your favorite recipes.

For this recipe you will need a glass, ceramic or BPA-free plastic container which will hold a minimum of 2 cups liquid; this will act as the form to shape the cheese.

Ingredients:

- 1 and ⅓ cup plain unsweetened soymilk with no additives (see pg. 8)
- ½ cup organic refined coconut oil
- ¼ cup tapioca flour
- ¼ cup nutritional yeast
- 4 and ½ tsp kappa carrageenan
- 1 T mellow white miso paste
- 1 T raw apple cider vinegar
- 1 T organic tomato paste
- 1 tsp sea salt or kosher salt
- 1 tsp onion powder
- ½ tsp dry ground mustard

Technique:

Measure the soymilk and let it come to room temperature (if chilled).

Remove the lid from the jar of coconut oil and place the jar in a microwave. Heat until the solid oil liquefies, about 30 seconds to 1 minute (this will depend upon the solidity of the coconut oil). Alternately, you can place the jar in about an inch of simmering water and melt the oil in the same manner. Measure ½ cup and pour into a blender.

Add the soymilk and the remaining ingredients to the blender and process on low speed until smooth, stopping to scrape down the sides of the blender as necessary with a rubber/silicone spatula.

Transfer the mixture to a saucepan and cook over medium-low heat, slowly and continuously stirring with a flexible rubber/silicone spatula and scraping the sides and bottom of the saucepan as necessary. Increase stirring speed as the mixture thickens and begins to form curds. Stir vigorously until the mixture becomes very thick, smooth and glossy (if using non-stick cookware, the cheese should pull away from the sides of the pan).

Now quickly transfer the melted cheese to the container but do not attempt to smooth the surface (the cheese will be too sticky); let the cheese settle on its own, or rap the container sharply on your work surface to help the cheese settle. Let the cheese cool at room temperature for about 20 minutes. Cover with plastic wrap, making sure the wrap comes into contact with the surface of the cheese and refrigerate for a minimum of 6 hours or until completely chilled and very firm.

When the cheese has been completely chilled and firmed, invert the container and tap sharply to remove (if necessary, carefully run a table knife around the inside perimeter to loosen). Wrap the cheese snugly in a paper towel and then wrap tightly in plastic wrap or seal in a zip-lock bag. Refrigerate for 24 hours. The paper towel will absorb any moisture released from the cheese during refrigeration and contribute to a firmer, drier texture.

Remove the paper towel and slice or shred as needed. Store the cheese in the refrigerator wrapped in a dry paper towel and then plastic wrap or a zip-lock bag (squeeze out as much air as possible before sealing). Replace the paper towel every few days.

Gloucester with Onions and Chives

Gloucester is a firm cheddar with a savory onion and chive flavor. Slice and serve with your favorite crackers. Thin slices add a gourmet touch to cold sandwiches or when melted on burgers or other grilled sandwiches.

For this recipe you will need a glass, ceramic or BPA-free plastic container which will hold a minimum of 2 cups liquid; this will act as the form to shape the cheese.

Ingredients:

- 1 and ⅓ cup plain unsweetened soymilk with no additives (see pg. 8)
- ½ cup organic refined coconut oil
- ¼ cup tapioca flour
- ¼ cup nutritional yeast
- 4 and ½ tsp kappa carrageenan
- 1 T mellow white miso paste
- 2 tsp raw apple cider vinegar
- 2 tsp organic tomato paste
- 1 tsp sea salt or kosher salt
- ½ tsp dry ground mustard
- 1 T freeze-dried chives
- 1 T dried minced onion

Technique:

Measure the soymilk and let it come to room temperature (if chilled).

Remove the lid from the jar of coconut oil and place the jar in a microwave. Heat until the solid oil liquefies, about 30 seconds to 1 minute (this will depend upon the solidity of the coconut oil). Alternately, you can place the jar in about an inch of simmering water and melt the oil in the same manner. Measure ½ cup and pour into a blender.

Add the soymilk and the remaining ingredients to the blender and process on low speed until smooth, stopping to scrape down the sides of the blender as necessary with a rubber/silicone spatula.

Transfer the mixture to a saucepan and cook over medium-low heat, slowly and continuously stirring with a flexible rubber/silicone spatula and scraping the sides and bottom of the saucepan as necessary. Increase stirring speed as the mixture thickens and begins to form curds. Stir vigorously until the mixture becomes very thick, smooth and glossy (if using non-stick cookware, the cheese should pull away from the sides of the pan).

Now quickly transfer the melted cheese to the container but do not attempt to smooth the surface (the cheese will be too sticky); let the cheese settle on its own, or rap the container sharply on your work surface to help the cheese settle. Let the cheese cool at room temperature for about 20 minutes. Cover with plastic wrap, making sure the wrap comes into contact with the surface of the cheese and refrigerate for a minimum of 6 hours or until completely chilled and very firm.

When the cheese has been completely chilled and firmed, invert the container and tap sharply to remove (if necessary, carefully run a table knife around the inside perimeter to loosen). Wrap the cheese snugly in a paper towel and then wrap tightly in plastic wrap or seal in a zip-lock bag. Refrigerate for 24 hours. The paper towel will absorb any moisture released from the cheese during refrigeration and contribute to a firmer, drier texture.

Remove the paper towel and slice or shred as needed. Store the cheese in the refrigerator wrapped in a dry paper towel and then plastic wrap or a zip-lock bag (squeeze out as much air as possible before sealing). Replace the paper towel every few days.

Harvest Smoked Cheddar

Harvest Smoked Cheddar is a firm cheese with a golden color, mild acidity and rich smoky flavor. Thin slices are ideal for cold sandwiches or for melting on burgers or other grilled sandwiches. This cheese can also be finely shredded and used in your favorite recipes.

For this recipe you will need a glass, ceramic or BPA-free plastic container which will hold a minimum of 2 cups liquid; this will act as the form to shape the cheese.

Ingredients:

- 1 and ⅓ cup plain unsweetened soymilk with no additives (see pg. 8)
- ½ cup organic refined coconut oil
- ¼ cup tapioca flour
- ¼ cup nutritional yeast
- 4 and ½ tsp kappa carrageenan
- 1 T mellow white miso paste
- 1 T liquid smoke
- 2 tsp organic tomato paste
- 1 tsp raw apple cider vinegar
- 1 tsp sea salt or kosher salt
- 1 tsp onion powder
- ½ tsp dry ground mustard

Technique:

Measure the soymilk and let it come to room temperature (if chilled).

Remove the lid from the jar of coconut oil and place the jar in a microwave. Heat until the solid oil liquefies, about 30 seconds to 1 minute (this will depend upon the solidity of the coconut oil). Alternately, you can place the jar in about an inch of simmering water and melt the oil in the same manner. Measure ½ cup and pour into a blender.

Add the soymilk and the remaining ingredients to the blender and process on low speed until smooth, stopping to scrape down the sides of the blender as necessary with a rubber/silicone spatula.

Transfer the mixture to a saucepan and cook over medium-low heat, slowly and continuously stirring with a flexible rubber/silicone spatula and scraping the sides and bottom of the saucepan as necessary. Increase stirring speed as the mixture thickens and begins to form curds. Stir vigorously until the mixture becomes very thick, smooth and glossy (if using non-stick cookware, the cheese should pull away from the sides of the pan).

Now quickly transfer the melted cheese to the container but do not attempt to smooth the surface (the cheese will be too sticky); let the cheese settle on its own, or rap the container sharply on your work surface to help the cheese settle. Let the cheese cool at room temperature for about 20 minutes. Cover with plastic wrap, making sure the wrap comes into contact with the surface of the cheese and refrigerate for a minimum of 6 hours or until completely chilled and very firm.

When the cheese has been completely chilled and firmed, invert the container and tap sharply to remove (if necessary, carefully run a table knife around the inside perimeter to loosen). Wrap the cheese snugly in a paper towel and then wrap tightly in plastic wrap or seal in a zip-lock bag. Refrigerate for 24 hours. The paper towel will absorb any moisture released from the cheese during refrigeration and contribute to a firmer, drier texture.

Remove the paper towel and slice or shred as needed. Store the cheese in the refrigerator wrapped in a dry paper towel and then plastic wrap or a zip-lock bag (squeeze out as much air as possible before sealing). Replace the paper towel every few days.

Chipotle Smoked Cheddar

Chipotle Smoked Cheddar is a zesty cheese with a smoky and peppery flavor. Thin slices liven up cold sandwiches and are superb for melting on burgers or other grilled sandwiches. Chipotle Smoked Cheddar can also be finely shredded and used in your favorite recipes.

To prepare this cheese, follow the recipe for Harvest Smoked Cheddar (pg. 58) and replace the 2 tsp tomato paste with 1 tsp chipotle chili powder.

Brie and Camembert

Brie is a soft, spreadable table cheese with a rich, buttery flavor. Camembert is very similar but with deeper, earthy undertones. Both cheeses are excellent when served at room temperature with fresh fruit and crackers or they can be baked "en croûte" (wrapped in flaky puff pastry with optional toppings and baked until melted).

For this recipe you will need a round glass, ceramic or BPA-free plastic container which will hold a minimum of 2 cups liquid; this will act as the form to shape the wheel of cheese. Line the form with cheesecloth or plastic wrap with excess hanging over the edge. This will help lift the cheese from the form after firming.

Ingredients:

- 1 and ⅓ cup plain unsweetened soymilk with no additives (see pg. 8)
- ½ cup organic refined coconut oil
- ¼ cup tapioca flour plus extra for dusting the exterior of the cheese
- 1 T nutritional yeast
- 1 T mellow white miso paste
- 1 tsp kappa carrageenan
- 1 tsp white truffle oil (for Camembert)
- 2 tsp raw apple cider vinegar
- 1 tsp sea salt or kosher salt

Technique:

Measure the soymilk and let it come to room temperature (if chilled).

Remove the lid from the jar of coconut oil and place the jar in a microwave. Heat until the solid oil liquefies, about 30 seconds to 1 minute (this will depend upon the solidity of the coconut oil). Alternately, you can place the jar in about an inch of simmering water and melt the oil in the same manner. Measure ½ cup and pour into a blender.

Add the soymilk and the remaining ingredients to the blender and process on low speed until smooth, stopping to scrape down the sides of the blender as necessary with a rubber/silicone spatula.

Transfer the mixture to a saucepan and cook over medium-low heat, slowly and continuously stirring with a flexible rubber/silicone spatula and scraping the sides and bottom of the saucepan as necessary. Increase stirring speed as the mixture thickens and begins to form curds. Keep stirring vigorously until the mixture becomes bubbly, smooth and glossy.

Now quickly transfer the melted cheese to the container. Let the cheese cool at room temperature for about 20 minutes. Refrigerate uncovered for a minimum of 6 hours.

Remove the cheese from the container by lifting the cheesecloth or plastic wrap. Discard the cheesecloth or plastic wrap. Handle the cheese carefully as it will be soft and rather sticky. For Brie (or Camembert) en Croûte, proceed to the following recipe.

Otherwise, generously dust the cheese on all sides with tapioca flour. This will help dry the surface and reduce stickiness. Set the cheese on a parchment lined plate or wire rack with the driest side on the bottom (the side that was exposed to air while refrigerating). Place the cheese in the refrigerator to air-dry for 8 hours. This will help create a "rind".

Let the cheese come to room temperature before serving. Store the cheese in the refrigerator in a zip-lock bag or securely wrapped in plastic wrap.

Brie (or Camembert) en Croûte
with Caramelized Mushrooms, Onions and Walnuts

Rich and buttery Brie (or Camembert) is baked in a puff pastry crust with caramelized mushrooms, onions and walnuts. This elegant appetizer is sure to impress. If desired, the filling can be replaced with fruit preserves, such as fig or apricot and any nuts that suit your fancy.

Ingredients:

- 1 round of Brie or Camembert (pg. 60)
- 1 sheet dairy and egg-free frozen puff pastry dough (e.g., Pepperidge Farm™)
- 1 T Better Butter (pg. 12)
- 4 large white button or cremini mushrooms (about 4 oz.)
- ½ medium onion, sliced thin and then chopped
- ¼ cup chopped walnuts (optional)
- ¼ tsp dried thyme
- a few pinches of salt and coarse ground black pepper
- a splash of dry white wine (e.g., Chardonnay, Sauvignon Blanc)

Technique:

Prepare the Brie or Camembert according to the directions. Let the cheese come to room temperature while the puff pastry dough thaws for about 30 to 40 minutes. Preheat the oven to 400°F.

In a skillet over medium heat, sauté the onions, mushrooms and walnuts in the butter or margarine until the onions are translucent. Add the thyme, a sprinkle of salt and pepper and the splash of optional wine and continue to sauté until the liquid has evaporated and the mushrooms and onions are browned nicely. Set aside to cool.

Lay out the puff pastry dough on a lightly oiled or parchment lined baking sheet and center the cheese in the middle. Top with the mushroom/onion/walnut mixture. Try to keep the mixture mounded on top of the cheese but if some falls to the sides, don't worry about it. Begin to fold the edges of the pastry dough over the mixture and cheese.

Bake until golden brown on top, about 30 to 35 minutes. Slice and serve immediately.

Pepper Jack

Pepper Jack has a piquant flavor that is wonderful for snacking with crackers. It can also be sliced and served on cold sandwiches, melted on grilled sandwiches or shredded and used in recipes. For a mild Monterey Jack, simply omit the green chili and red pepper. For this recipe you will need a glass, ceramic or BPA-free plastic container which will hold a minimum of 2 cups liquid; this will act as the form to shape the cheese.

Ingredients:

- 1 large jalapeno or Serrano chili
- 1 and ⅓ cup plain unsweetened soymilk with no additives (see pg. 8)
- ⅔ cup organic refined coconut oil
- ¼ cup tapioca flour
- 4 tsp kappa carrageenan
- 4 tsp nutritional yeast
- 2 tsp white wine vinegar
- 1 tsp sea salt or kosher salt
- ½ tsp onion powder
- 1 tsp red pepper flakes, divided in half

Technique:

Measure the soymilk and let it come to room temperature (if chilled).

Seed and finely mince 1 jalapeno or Serrano chili. Wear gloves if you have sensitive skin or be sure to wash your hands thoroughly after handling. Spray a small skillet with a little cooking oil spray and sauté the pepper until lightly browned. Be careful not to burn the pepper. Set aside.

Remove the lid from the jar of coconut oil and place the jar in a microwave. Heat until the solid oil liquefies, about 30 seconds to 1 minute (this will depend upon the solidity of the coconut oil). Alternately, you can place the jar in about an inch of simmering water and melt the oil in the same manner. Measure ⅔ cup and pour into a blender.

Add the soymilk and the remaining ingredients to the blender EXCEPT for the reserved green chili pepper. Also add ½ tsp red pepper flakes (reserve the other ½ tsp).

Process the contents on low speed until smooth, stopping to scrape down the sides of the blender as necessary with a rubber/silicone spatula.

Add the green chili and reserved red pepper flakes and pulse the mixture once or twice to combine. If you desire more heat, add additional red pepper flakes.

Transfer the mixture to a saucepan and cook over medium-low heat, slowly and continuously stirring with a flexible rubber/silicone spatula and scraping the sides and bottom of the saucepan as necessary. Increase stirring speed as the mixture thickens and begins to form curds. Stir vigorously until the mixture becomes very thick, smooth and glossy (if using non-stick cookware, the cheese should pull away from the sides of the pan).

Now quickly transfer the melted cheese to the container but do not attempt to smooth the surface (the cheese will be too sticky); let the cheese settle on its own, or rap the container sharply on your work surface to help the cheese settle. Let the cheese cool for 20 minutes until the surface has set. Cover with plastic wrap, making sure the wrap comes in contact with the surface of the cheese and refrigerate for a minimum of 6 hours or until completely chilled and very firm.

When the cheese has been completely chilled and firmed, invert the container and tap sharply to remove (if necessary, carefully run a table knife around the inside perimeter to loosen). Wrap the cheese snugly in a paper towel and then wrap tightly in plastic wrap or seal in a zip-lock bag. Refrigerate for 24 hours. The paper towel will absorb any moisture released from the cheese during refrigeration and contribute to a firmer, drier texture.

Remove the paper towel and slice or shred as needed. Store the cheese in the refrigerator wrapped in a dry paper towel and then plastic wrap or a zip-lock bag (squeeze out as much air as possible before sealing). Replace the paper towel every few days.

Firm Mozzarella

Firm mozzarella is a mildly acidic cheese with a very mild flavor. Its solid texture makes it excellent for fine shredding and melting.

For this recipe you will need a glass, ceramic or BPA-free plastic container which will hold a minimum of 2 cups liquid; this will act as the form to shape the cheese.

Ingredients:

- 1 and ⅓ cup plain unsweetened soymilk with no additives (see pg. 8)
- ⅔ cup organic refined coconut oil
- ¼ cup tapioca flour
- 4 tsp kappa carrageenan
- 1 T fresh lemon juice
- 1 tsp white wine vinegar
- ¾ tsp sea salt or kosher salt
- ½ tsp onion powder

Technique:

Measure the soymilk and let it come to room temperature (if chilled).

Remove the lid from the jar of coconut oil and place the jar in a microwave. Heat until the solid oil liquefies, about 30 seconds to 1 minute (this will depend upon the solidity of the coconut oil). Alternately, you can place the jar in about an inch of simmering water and melt the oil in the same manner. Measure ⅔ cup and pour into a blender.

Add the soymilk and the remaining ingredients to the blender and process on low speed until smooth, stopping to scrape down the sides of the blender as necessary with a rubber/silicone spatula.

Transfer the mixture to a saucepan and cook over medium-low heat, slowly and continuously stirring with a flexible rubber/silicone spatula and scraping the sides and bottom of the saucepan as necessary. Increase stirring speed as the mixture thickens and begins to form curds. Stir vigorously until the mixture becomes very thick, smooth and glossy (if using non-stick cookware, the cheese should pull away from the sides of the pan).

Now quickly transfer the melted cheese to the container but do not attempt to smooth the surface (it will be too sticky); let the cheese settle on its own, or rap the container sharply on your work surface to help the cheese settle. Let the cheese cool at room temperature for about 20 minutes. Cover with plastic wrap, making sure the wrap comes in contact with the surface of the cheese and refrigerate for a minimum of 6 hours or until completely chilled and very firm.

When the cheese has been completely chilled and firmed, invert the container and tap sharply to remove (if necessary, carefully run a table knife around the inside perimeter to loosen). Wrap the cheese snugly in a paper towel and then wrap tightly in plastic wrap or seal in a zip-lock bag. Refrigerate for 24 hours. The paper towel will absorb any moisture released from the cheese during refrigeration and contribute to a firmer, drier texture.

Remove the paper towel and slice or shred as needed. Store the cheese in the refrigerator wrapped in a dry paper towel and then plastic wrap or a zip-lock bag (squeeze out as much air as possible before sealing). Replace the paper towel every few days.

Fresh Mozzarella

Fresh Mozzarella is a semi-soft, mildly acidic cheese with a very mild flavor. It's prepared in the same manner as Firm Mozzarella, but rather than being shaped in a block form, it's scooped into round balls and chilled in a brine solution. Fresh Mozzarella is a traditional component of Insalata Caprese (pg. 69), a salad comprised of tomatoes, onions, fresh basil and olive oil. It also melts nicely when sliced and baked on bruschetta or pizza.

For the brine, combine in a sealable container and refrigerate until very cold:

- 4 cups water
- 2 tsp sea salt or kosher salt

For the cheese you will need:

- 1 and ⅓ cup plain unsweetened soymilk with no additives (see pg. 8)
- ⅔ cup organic refined coconut oil
- ¼ cup tapioca flour
- 1 T kappa carrageenan
- 1 T fresh lemon juice
- 1 tsp white wine vinegar
- ¾ tsp sea salt or kosher salt
- ½ tsp onion powder

Technique:

Measure the soymilk and let it come to room temperature (if chilled).

Remove the lid from the jar of coconut oil and place the jar in a microwave. Heat until the solid oil liquefies, about 30 seconds to 1 minute (this will depend upon the solidity of the coconut oil). Alternately, you can place the jar in about an inch of simmering water and melt the oil in the same manner. Measure ⅔ cup and pour into a blender.

Add the soymilk and the remaining cheese ingredients to the blender (not the brine ingredients). Process the contents on low speed until smooth, stopping to scrape down the sides of the blender as necessary with a rubber/silicone spatula.

Transfer the mixture to a saucepan and cook over medium-low heat, slowly and continuously stirring with a flexible rubber/silicone spatula and scraping the sides and bottom of the saucepan as necessary. Increase stirring speed as the mixture thickens and begins to form curds. Stir vigorously until the mixture becomes very thick, smooth and glossy (if using non-stick cookware, the cheese should pull away from the sides of the pan). Remove the saucepan from the heat and place on a trivet or other heatproof surface near your work area.

With an ice cream scoop or ladle, scoop up the hot cheese mixture and, with a spoon in your opposite hand, scrape off any cheese that is hanging from the sides of the scoop back into the saucepan. This will help create more uniformly round balls of cheese. Add the scoop of cheese to the chilled brine. The exterior of the cheese ball will firm upon contact. Repeat with the remaining cheese mixture.

Refrigerate for several hours until the brine is re-chilled and the mozzarella balls have firmed (keep in mind that the cheese will still be very soft).

Drain with a slotted spoon and set on a paper towel to blot excess water before using in recipes. Stored in the brine, the mozzarella should keep for about 1 week in the refrigerator. Freezing is not recommended for this cheese.

Insalata Caprese
(Chef's Variation)

This is my own variation of the traditional Insalata Caprese. Here I've combined stewed tomatoes with sliced onions, fresh basil, fresh mozzarella, caperberries and balsamic vinaigrette for a cool and refreshing salad. This is one of my favorites and I think you'll enjoy it too. This salad needs to be prepared at least a day ahead to allow time for the salad ingredients to marinate, so plan accordingly.

Ingredients:

- 2 cans (14 oz. each) stewed tomatoes with the juice
- 1 small onion, thinly sliced
- 1 bunch fresh basil, chiffonade (sliced into ribbons)
- ⅔ cup balsamic vinaigrette
  or your favorite commercial balsamic vinaigrette
- Fresh Mozzarella (pg. 67), ¼-inch thick slices
- sea salt or kosher salt and coarse ground black pepper, to taste
- optional garnish: caperberries*

*Caperberries are the fruit of the Mediterranean caper bush, whereas capers are the small flower buds.

Technique:

Prepare the fresh mozzarella and refrigerate. In a large bowl or food storage container with a lid, combine all of the ingredients except the mozzarella. Cover and refrigerate overnight. To serve, spoon the salad into a serving bowl and top with slices of the mozzarella. Garnish with the optional caperberries and additional fresh basil if desired.

Tip: Try serving this salad over toasted crusty bread rounds or croutons; the crisp bread soaks up the flavorful juice and is absolutely delicious!

Smoked Provolone

Smoked Provolone is a firm Italian cheese with a smoky flavor that adds panache to cold sandwiches or when melted on burgers or grilled sandwiches. The firm texture of this cheese makes it easy to slice very thin, especially when using an electric deli slicer.

For this recipe you will need a glass, ceramic or BPA-free plastic container which will hold a minimum of 2 cups liquid; this will act as the form to shape the cheese.

Ingredients:

- 1 and ⅓ cup plain unsweetened soymilk with no additives (see pg. 8)
- ½ cup organic refined coconut oil
- ¼ cup tapioca flour
- 4 tsp kappa carrageenan
- 2 T mellow white miso paste
- 2 tsp liquid smoke
- ½ tsp sea salt or kosher salt
- ½ tsp onion powder
- ½ tsp white wine vinegar

Technique:

Measure the soymilk and let it come to room temperature (if chilled).

Remove the lid from the jar of coconut oil and place the jar in a microwave. Heat until the solid oil liquefies, about 30 seconds to 1 minute (this will depend upon the solidity of the coconut oil). Alternately, you can place the jar in about an inch of simmering water and melt the oil in the same manner. Measure ½ cup and pour into a blender.

Add the remaining ingredients to the blender and process on low speed until smooth, stopping to scrape down the sides of the blender as necessary with a rubber/silicone spatula.

Transfer the mixture to a medium saucepan and cook over medium-low heat, slowly and continuously stirring with a flexible rubber/silicone spatula and scraping the sides of the saucepan as necessary. Increase stirring speed as the mixture thickens and begins to form curds. Stir vigorously until the mixture becomes very thick, smooth and glossy (if using non-stick cookware, the cheese should pull away from the sides of the pan).

Now, immediately pour the melted cheese into the container but do not attempt to smooth the surface; let the cheese settle on its own, or rap the container sharply on your work surface to help the cheese settle. Let the cheese stand for 20 minutes until the surface has cooled and set. Cover with plastic wrap, making sure the wrap comes in contact with the surface of the cheese and refrigerate for a minimum of 6 hours or until completely chilled and very firm.

When the cheese has been completely chilled and firmed, invert the container and tap sharply to remove (if necessary, carefully run a table knife around the inside perimeter to loosen). Wrap the cheese snugly in a paper towel and then wrap tightly in plastic wrap or seal in a zip-lock bag. Refrigerate for 24 hours. The paper towel will absorb any moisture released from the cheese during refrigeration and contribute to a firmer, drier texture.

Remove the paper towel and slice or shred as needed. Store the cheese in the refrigerator wrapped in a dry paper towel and then plastic wrap or a zip-lock bag (squeeze out as much air as possible before sealing). Replace the paper towel every few days.

Dill Havarti

Dill Havarti is a creamy, buttery and moderately acidic, semi-firm table cheese. The dill adds a wonderful flavor without being overpowering. It's ideal for slicing and serving on crackers or cold sandwiches and superb for melting on grilled sandwiches.

For this recipe you will need a glass, ceramic or BPA-free plastic container which will hold a minimum of 2 cups liquid; this will act as the form to shape the cheese.

Ingredients:

- 1 and ⅓ cup plain unsweetened soymilk with no additives (see pg. 8)
- ⅔ cup organic refined coconut oil
- ¼ cup tapioca flour
- 4 tsp nutritional yeast
- 1 T kappa carrageenan
- 2 tsp fresh lemon juice
- 2 tsp white wine vinegar
- 1 tsp sea salt or kosher salt
- 1 T finely minced fresh dill, lightly packed

Technique:

Measure the soymilk and let it come to room temperature (if chilled).

Remove the lid from the jar of coconut oil and place the jar in a microwave. Heat until the solid oil liquefies, about 30 seconds to 1 minute (this will depend upon the solidity of the coconut oil). Alternately, you can place the jar in about an inch of simmering water and melt the oil in the same manner. Measure ⅔ cup and pour into a blender.

Add the soymilk and the remaining ingredients EXCEPT for the minced dill to the blender. Process the contents on low speed until smooth, stopping to scrape down the sides of the blender as necessary with a rubber/silicone spatula.

Transfer the mixture to a saucepan, add the minced dill and cook over medium-low heat, slowly and continuously stirring with a flexible rubber/silicone spatula and scraping the sides and bottom of the saucepan as necessary. Increase stirring speed as the mixture thickens and begins to form curds. Stir vigorously until the mixture becomes very thick, smooth and glossy (if using non-stick cookware, the cheese should pull away from the sides of the pan).

Now quickly transfer the melted cheese to the container but do not attempt to smooth the surface; let the cheese settle on its own, or rap the container sharply on your work surface to help the cheese settle. Let the cheese cool at room temperature for about 20 minutes.

Cover with plastic wrap, making sure the wrap comes in contact with the surface of the cheese and refrigerate for a minimum of 6 hours or until completely chilled and firm.

When the cheese has been completely chilled and firmed, invert the container and tap sharply to remove (if necessary, carefully run a table knife around the inside perimeter to loosen). Wrap the cheese snugly in a paper towel and then wrap tightly in plastic wrap or seal in a zip-lock bag. Refrigerate for 24 hours. The paper towel will absorb any moisture released from the cheese during refrigeration and contribute to a firmer, drier texture.

Remove the paper towel and slice or shred as needed. Store the cheese in the refrigerator wrapped in a dry paper towel and then plastic wrap or a zip-lock bag (squeeze out as much air as possible before sealing). Replace the paper towel every few days.

Variation: If you like the flavor of caraway, try replacing the dill with 1 teaspoon of caraway seed lightly crushed with a mortar and pestle. For a garlicky and peppery variation, replace the dill with 1 tablespoon of cracked black pepper and 2 tsp minced garlic (2 cloves).

Alpine Swiss

Alpine Swiss is a firm cheese with a mild, nutty flavor that is very reminiscent of dairy Swiss cheese. It can be thinly sliced and served on cold sandwiches, grilled and melted on hot sandwiches or shredded and used in recipes.

For this recipe you will need a glass, ceramic or BPA-free plastic container which will hold a minimum of 2 cups liquid; this will act as the form to shape the cheese.

Ingredients:

- 1 and ⅓ cup plain unsweetened soymilk with no additives (see pg. 8)
- ½ cup organic refined coconut oil
- ¼ cup tapioca flour
- 2 T dry sherry or dry white wine
- 4 tsp kappa carrageenan
- 3 T nutritional yeast
- 1 T sesame tahini
- 1 tsp sea salt or kosher salt
- 1 tsp dry ground mustard

Technique:

Measure the soymilk and let it come to room temperature (if chilled).

Remove the lid from the jar of coconut oil and place the jar in a microwave. Heat until the solid oil liquefies, about 30 seconds to 1 minute (this will depend upon the solidity of the coconut oil). Alternately, you can place the jar in about an inch of simmering water and melt the oil in the same manner. Measure ½ cup and pour into a blender.

Add the soymilk and the remaining ingredients to the blender and process on low speed until smooth, stopping to scrape down the sides of the blender as necessary with a rubber/silicone spatula.

Transfer the mixture to a saucepan and cook over medium-low heat, slowly and continuously stirring with a flexible rubber/silicone spatula and scraping the sides and bottom of the saucepan as necessary. Increase stirring speed as the mixture thickens and begins to form curds. Stir vigorously until the mixture becomes very thick, smooth and glossy (if using non-stick cookware, the cheese should pull away from the sides of the pan).

Now quickly transfer the melted cheese to the container but do not attempt to smooth the surface (the cheese will be too sticky); let the cheese settle on its own, or rap the container sharply on your work surface to help the cheese settle. Let the cheese cool at room temperature for about 20 minutes. Cover with plastic wrap, making sure the wrap comes in contact with the surface of the cheese and refrigerate for a minimum of 6 hours or until completely chilled and very firm.

When the cheese has been completely chilled and firmed, invert the container and tap sharply to remove (if necessary, carefully run a table knife around the inside perimeter to loosen). Wrap the cheese snugly in a paper towel and then wrap tightly in plastic wrap or seal in a zip-lock bag. Refrigerate for 24 hours. The paper towel will absorb any moisture released from the cheese during refrigeration and contribute to a firmer, drier texture.

Remove the paper towel and slice or shred as needed. Store the cheese in the refrigerator wrapped in a dry paper towel and then plastic wrap or a zip-lock bag (squeeze out as much air as possible before sealing). Replace the paper towel every few days.

Muenster Cheese

Muenster is a cheese from the United States, not to be confused with the French variety, Munster. This non-dairy version has a semi-firm texture with an orange "rind" and a mild, buttery flavor. The coloration of the "rind" is created by rubbing the exterior of the cheese with sweet paprika. Slices are ideal for cold sandwiches and for melting on burgers or other grilled sandwiches.

For this recipe you will need a glass, ceramic or BPA-free plastic container which will hold a minimum of 2 cups liquid; this will act as the form to shape the cheese.

Ingredients:

- 1 tsp sweet paprika (to color the exterior)
- 1 and ⅓ cup plain unsweetened soymilk with no additives (see pg. 8)
- ⅔ cup organic refined coconut oil
- ¼ cup tapioca flour
- 1 T kappa carrageenan
- 2 T nutritional yeast
- 2 tsp raw apple cider vinegar
- 1 tsp sea salt or kosher salt
- ¼ tsp onion powder
- ¼ tsp dry ground mustard

Technique:

Measure the soymilk and let it come to room temperature (if chilled).

Lightly spray the cheese form with vegetable oil. Add the paprika and turn the form side to side and back and forth to dust the interior with the spice. It's not essential to coat it evenly, just do the best you can. Discard any loose spice by inverting and tapping the container. Set aside.

Remove the lid from the jar of coconut oil and place the jar in a microwave. Heat until the solid oil liquefies, about 30 seconds to 1 minute (this will depend upon the solidity of the coconut oil). Alternately, you can place the jar in about an inch of simmering water and melt the oil in the same manner. Measure ⅔ cup and pour into a blender.

Add the soymilk and the remaining ingredients to the blender and process on low speed until smooth, stopping to scrape down the sides of the blender as necessary with a rubber/silicone spatula.

Transfer the mixture to a saucepan and cook over medium-low heat, slowly and continuously stirring with a flexible rubber/silicone spatula and scraping the sides and bottom of the saucepan as necessary. Increase stirring speed as the mixture thickens and begins to form curds. Stir vigorously until the mixture becomes very thick, smooth and glossy (if using non-stick cookware, the cheese should pull away from the sides of the pan).

Now quickly transfer the melted cheese to the container but do not attempt to smooth the surface (the cheese will be too sticky); let the cheese settle on its own, or rap the container sharply on your work surface to help the cheese settle. Let the cheese cool at room temperature for about 20 minutes. Cover with plastic wrap, making sure the wrap comes in contact with the surface of the cheese and refrigerate for a minimum of 6 hours or until completely chilled and very firm.

When the cheese has been completely chilled and firmed, invert the container and tap sharply to remove (if necessary, carefully run a table knife around the inside perimeter to loosen). Gently rub the cheese to distribute the paprika evenly.

Wrap the cheese snugly in a paper towel and then wrap tightly in plastic wrap or seal in a zip-lock bag. Refrigerate for 24 hours. The paper towel will absorb any moisture released from the cheese during refrigeration and contribute to a firmer, drier texture.

Remove the paper towel and slice or shred as needed. Store the cheese in the refrigerator wrapped in a dry paper towel and then plastic wrap or a zip-lock bag (squeeze out as much air as possible before sealing). Replace the paper towel every few days.

Smoked Gouda

Gouda is an iconic Dutch cheese. My dairy-free version produces a firm table cheese with a distinctive smoke flavor which is very reminiscent of dairy smoked Gouda. It's wonderful for snacking with crackers but adds a gourmet touch when sliced for cold sandwiches or melted on grilled sandwiches.

For this recipe you will need a glass, ceramic or BPA-free plastic container which will hold a minimum of 2 cups liquid; this will act as the form to shape the cheese.

Ingredients:

- 1 and ⅓ cup plain unsweetened soymilk with no additives (see pg. 8)
- ⅔ cup organic refined coconut oil
- ¼ cup tapioca flour
- 2 T nutritional yeast
- 4 tsp kappa carrageenan
- 2 tsp liquid smoke
- 1 tsp vegan Worcestershire sauce
- ¾ tsp sea salt or kosher salt
- ½ tsp onion powder

Technique:

Measure the soymilk and let it come to room temperature (if chilled).

Remove the lid from the jar of coconut oil and place the jar in a microwave. Heat until the solid oil liquefies, about 30 seconds to 1 minute (this will depend upon the solidity of the coconut oil). Alternately, you can place the jar in about an inch of simmering water and melt the oil in the same manner. Measure ⅔ cup and pour into a blender.

Add the soymilk and the remaining ingredients to the blender and process on low speed until smooth, stopping to scrape down the sides of the blender as necessary with a rubber/silicone spatula.

Transfer the mixture to a saucepan and cook over medium-low heat, slowly and continuously stirring with a flexible rubber/silicone spatula and scraping the sides and bottom of the saucepan as necessary. Increase stirring speed as the mixture thickens and begins to form curds. Stir vigorously until the mixture becomes very thick, smooth and glossy (if using non-stick cookware, the cheese should pull away from the sides of the pan).

Now quickly transfer the melted cheese to the container but do not attempt to smooth the surface (it will be too sticky); let the cheese settle on its own, or rap the container sharply on your work surface to help the cheese settle.

Let the cheese cool at room temperature for about 20 minutes. Cover with plastic wrap, making sure the wrap comes in contact with the surface of the cheese and refrigerate for a minimum of 6 hours or until completely chilled and very firm.

When the cheese has been completely chilled and firmed, invert the container and tap sharply to remove (if necessary, carefully run a table knife around the inside perimeter to loosen). Wrap the cheese snugly in a paper towel and then wrap tightly in plastic wrap or seal in a zip-lock bag. Refrigerate for 24 hours. The paper towel will absorb any moisture released from the cheese during refrigeration and contribute to a firmer, drier texture.

Remove the paper towel and slice or shred as needed. Store the cheese in the refrigerator wrapped in a dry paper towel and then plastic wrap or a zip-lock bag (squeeze out as much air as possible before sealing). Replace the paper towel every few days.

Smoked Gouda, Spinach and Artichoke Dip

Smoked Gouda cheese and Golden Parmesan is blended with a creamy and chunky purée of spinach and artichokes and then baked to perfection.

Ingredients:

- 2 T vegetable oil
- 1 small onion, chopped
- 2 tsp minced garlic (2 cloves)
- 1 pkg (10 oz.) frozen spinach
- 1 can (14 oz.) artichoke hearts, rinsed and drained well
- 1 cup shredded Smoked Gouda (pg. 78)
- ½ cup Sour Cream (pg. 28)
- ¼ cup No-Eggy Mayo (pg. 133)
- 2 T Grated Parmesan (pg. 89)
- sea salt or kosher salt and coarse ground black pepper, to taste

Technique:

Thaw and press the spinach to remove as much liquid as possible (a tofu press is ideal for this).

Preheat the oven to 350°F and lightly oil a shallow baking dish.

In a skillet over medium heat, sauté the onion in the vegetable oil until the onion is translucent. Add the garlic and spinach. Sauté until the onion begins to lightly brown. This will take several minutes. Transfer to a food processor. Add the artichoke hearts to the food processor with the spinach/onion/garlic mixture. Pulse a few times to coarsely chop but do not purée.

Transfer to a mixing bowl; add the cheese, sour cream, mayonnaise and parmesan and stir thoroughly to combine. Season the mixture with salt and pepper to taste. Transfer to the baking dish and bake uncovered for 30 minutes.

Now, set the oven on "broil" and broil for an additional 3 or 4 minutes or until lightly brown on top. Serve hot with crackers, bread or crudités. To keep warm for special occasions, transfer to a chafing dish and heat over a low flame.

To serve in a bread bowl, tear chunks from the interior of a round loaf of crusty bread to hollow out the loaf. Reserve the bread chunks for dipping. Wrap the bread bowl in foil and heat in a warm oven. Transfer the cheese mixture to the warm bread bowl and serve immediately; otherwise keep warm in the oven until ready to serve.

Tofu-Based Cheeses

Mediterranean Herbed Feta

This tofu-based cheese is simple to make and is reminiscent of dairy feta cheese in both taste and texture. It has a tangy, slightly salty flavor and is wonderful for topping Mediterranean salads or for using in recipes such as Spanakopita in Fillo Cups (recipe follows). Be sure to use EXTRA-FIRM water-packed block tofu for the proper dry, crumbly texture. This recipe yields about 8 oz.

Ingredients:

- ½ block (7 oz.) extra-firm water-packed tofu (do not use silken tofu)
- ¼ cup organic refined coconut oil
- 1 T plus 1 tsp fresh lemon juice
- 1 T white wine vinegar
- 1 and ½ tsp sea salt or kosher salt
- ¼ tsp onion powder
- 1 tsp dried basil
- ½ tsp each dried marjoram and oregano

Technique:

Drain and press the tofu until it is not releasing any more liquid. (See Preparing Tofu for Recipes, pg. 10) It is essential to dry the tofu as much as possible for the proper texture. Crumble the tofu into a food processor.

Remove the metal lid from the jar of coconut oil and place the jar in a microwave. Heat just until the solid oil liquefies, about 30 seconds to 1 minute (this will depend upon the solidity of the coconut oil). Alternately, you can place the jar in about an inch of simmering water and melt the oil in the same manner. Measure ¼ cup and add to the food processor with the remaining ingredients EXCEPT for the dried herbs. Process the contents until very smooth.

Add the dried herbs and pulse to combine. Line a small food storage container with plastic wrap, being sure to leave some excess wrap hanging over the sides. Transfer the cheese mixture to the container. Pack the mixture with the back of a spoon and smooth the surface as best you can. Cover with a lid or additional plastic wrap and refrigerate for a minimum of 12 hours. This will ensure that the coconut oil has completely solidified. Once firmed, lift the cheese from the container and crumble as needed. When using as a topping for salads, toss the salad first with the dressing and then add the crumbles. Store in a zip-lock bag or wrapped tightly in plastic wrap in the refrigerator.

Spanakopita in Fillo Cups
(Greek Spinach and Feta Appetizers)

These savory bite-size appetizers are very easy to make. The spinach and feta filling is spooned into individual mini fillo cups and then baked. Mini fillo cups can be found in the frozen section of most supermarkets where frozen pie and pastry crusts are located.

Ingredients

- 1 package (10 oz.) frozen chopped spinach, thawed
- ½ tsp coarse ground black pepper
- 2 T olive oil
- 4 oz. Mediterranean Herbed Feta (pg. 81), crumbled
- 1 pkg. (15 count) frozen mini fillo cups

Technique:

Position a rack in the center of the oven and preheat to 350°F.

Place the thawed spinach in a wire-mesh strainer and place over a sink. Use your hands or the back of a spoon to squeeze the excess water out of the spinach. Try to remove as much moisture as possible. A tofu press is also very effective for pressing spinach.

Place the spinach in a mixing bowl; add the pepper, olive oil and feta cheese and mix thoroughly.

Spoon the spinach and cheese mixture into the frozen fillo cups. Place the fillo cups onto the baking sheet and bake for 15 minutes. Serve immediately.

Chèvre with Basil Pesto and Sundried Tomato

This tangy tofu-based chèvre is flavored with sun-dried tomatoes and dairy-free basil pesto. It makes a flavorful spread for crackers or crusty bread. A food processor is recommended for efficient processing. This recipe yields about 8 oz.

Ingredients:

- ½ block (7 oz.) extra-firm water packed tofu (do not use silken tofu)
- 3 T organic refined coconut oil
- 2 T fresh lemon juice
- 1 tsp sea salt of kosher salt
- ½ tsp onion powder
- 2 T finely chopped sun-dried tomatoes (dry or oil packed)
- 2 T Basil Pesto (pg. 90)

Technique:

Drain and press the tofu until it is not releasing any more liquid. (See Preparing Tofu for Recipes, pg. 10) Crumble the tofu into a food processor.

Remove the metal lid from the jar of coconut oil and place the jar in a microwave. Heat just until the solid oil liquefies, about 30 seconds to 1 minute (this will depend upon the solidity of the coconut oil). Alternately, you can place the jar in about an inch of simmering water and melt the oil in the same manner. Measure 3 tablespoons and add to the food processor. Add the lemon juice, onion powder and salt.

Process the contents until completely smooth. Transfer the mixture to a container with a lid, cover and refrigerate overnight. Now prepare the basil pesto so it will be ready the following day.

The following day, finely chop the sun-dried tomatoes and set aside (if the tomatoes were packed in oil, be sure to blot them thoroughly with a paper towel to remove the excess oil).

Lay a sheet of wax paper onto your work surface and scoop the cheese mixture onto the wax paper. Sprinkle the mixture with the chopped sun-dried tomatoes and spoon teaspoons of the pesto randomly onto the cheese.

Now, with your fingers, gently form the cheese into a log shape, pressing the tomatoes and pesto into the cheese. Don't worry about shaping perfection; the foil will shape the cheese into a log when rolled. Roll the mixture, like a tootsie roll, inside the wax paper and twist the ends tightly. Place the roll back in the refrigerator for a couple of hours to re-firm. To serve, simply remove the wax paper wrapper and place on a serving plate.

Gorgonzola

Dairy gorgonzola is a variety of Italian blue cheese. It has a salty flavor and strong bite which is produced by the mold Penicillium glaucum. This mold also gives gorgonzola its characteristic blue-green veins. While this tofu-based version doesn't capture the ripened quality of dairy gorgonzola exactly, it has a tangy flavor that is wonderful when served on crackers or as a crumbled topping on salads, pizza, risotto or polenta.

Be sure to use EXTRA-FIRM water-packed block tofu for the proper dry, crumbly texture. A food processor is recommended for efficient processing. You will also need a glass, ceramic or BPA-free plastic container which will hold a minimum of 1 cup liquid; this will act as the form to shape the cheese. Line the form with plastic wrap with excess hanging over the edge. This will help lift the cheese from the form after firming. This recipe yields about 8 oz.

Ingredients:
- ½ block (7 oz.) extra-firm water-packed tofu (do not use silken tofu)
- ¼ cup organic refined coconut oil
- 2 T mellow white miso paste
- 1 T plus 1 tsp white wine vinegar
- 2 tsp fresh lemon juice
- 1 tsp sea salt or kosher salt
- 1 tsp onion powder
- ¼ tsp garlic powder
- ⅛ tsp blue-green algae powder (spirulina)

Technique:

Drain and press the tofu until it is not releasing any more liquid. (See Preparing Tofu for Recipes, pg. 10) It is essential to dry the tofu as much as possible for the proper texture. Crumble the tofu into a food processor.

Remove the metal lid from the jar of coconut oil and place the jar in a microwave. Heat just until the solid oil liquefies, about 30 seconds to 1 minute (this will depend upon the solidity of the coconut oil). Alternately, you can place the jar in about an inch of simmering water and melt the oil in the same manner. Measure ¼ cup and add to the food processor with the remaining ingredients EXCEPT for the algae powder. Process the contents until very smooth.

Transfer the cheese mixture to the container. Dot the cheese in several spots with the algae powder and fold (rather than stir) the cheese over a few times to create swirls of blue-green color. Pack the mixture with the back of a spoon and smooth the surface as best you can. Cover with a lid or additional plastic wrap and refrigerate for a minimum of 12 hours. This will ensure that the coconut oil has completely solidified.

Lift the cheese from the container and slice or crumble as needed. Store the cheese wrapped in plastic wrap or in a zip-lock bag in the refrigerator. Because this cheese is made with miso, a fermented product, the flavor will continue to develop during refrigeration.

Ricotta

Ricotta is superb for stuffed pasta shells, manicotti or lasagna.

Ingredients:

- 1 block (14 oz.) firm or extra-firm water-packed tofu (do not use silken tofu)
- 2 T olive oil
- 1 T fresh lemon juice
- 1 tsp nutritional yeast
- ½ tsp onion powder
- ½ tsp sea salt or kosher salt
- ¼ tsp ground white pepper
- 1 tsp each of dried basil, parsley, and oregano (optional)
- plain unsweetened soymilk to thin to desired consistency, if necessary

Technique:

Drain and press the tofu until it is not releasing any more liquid. (See Preparing Tofu for Recipes, pg. 10)

In a large mixing bowl, mash the tofu with a fork. Add the remaining ingredients and mix thoroughly. Use a scant amount of soymilk if necessary to thin to desired consistency. Refrigerate in a covered container until ready to use.

Spinach Ricotta

Thaw 5 oz. of frozen spinach (½ of a 10 oz. pkg.) Press the spinach in a fine-mesh strainer using the back of large spoon (or use a tofu press) to remove as much moisture as possible. Add the spinach to a food processor and pulse to purée. Add the puréed spinach to the ricotta in a bowl and stir to blend. Spinach ricotta is delicious in stuffed pasta shells, manicotti and lasagna.

Cottage Cheese

This creamy non-dairy cottage cheese is very similar in both taste and texture to its dairy counterpart. Try stirring in some drained pineapple tidbits; or try minced fresh chives for a savory flavor.

Ingredients:

- 1 block (about 14 oz.) firm/extra-firm water-packed tofu (do not use silken tofu)
- ⅔ cup Light Cream (pg. 18)
- ⅓ cup No-Eggy Mayo (pg. 133)
- ½ tsp sea salt or kosher salt

Technique:

Press the tofu to remove as much moisture as possible. In a mixing bowl, mash the tofu with a fork but leave a little texture.

Whisk the light cream, mayonnaise and salt together in a separate small bowl.

Add the mixture to the crumbled tofu and mix thoroughly (if the tofu seems a bit saucy at first, don't worry, it will absorb a substantial amount of moisture after several minutes).

Refrigerate for a few hours to chill before serving. If the cottage cheese appears dry after chilling, stir in small amounts of non-dairy milk to remoisten.

Garlic Herb Gournay

This garlicky, semi-soft cheese makes a flavorful spread for crackers or crusty bread. The texture is similar to Boursin™, a trademarked brand of Gournay cheese. A food processor is recommended for efficient processing. This recipe yields about 8 oz.

Ingredients:

- ½ block (7 oz.) extra-firm water-packed tofu (do not use silken tofu)
- 3 T organic refined coconut oil
- 2 T fresh lemon juice
- 3 cloves garlic, chopped
- 2 tsp raw apple cider vinegar
- 2 tsp dried parsley
- 2 tsp dried minced chives
- 1 tsp dried basil
- 1 tsp fine sea salt or kosher salt
- 1 tsp onion powder
- ½ tsp coarse ground black pepper
- ¼ tsp dried thyme leaves

Technique:

Drain and press the tofu until it is not releasing any more liquid. (See Preparing Tofu for Recipes, pg. 10) Crumble the tofu into a food processor.

Remove the metal lid from the jar of coconut oil and place the jar in a microwave. Heat just until the solid oil liquefies, about 30 seconds to 1 minute (this will depend upon the solidity of the coconut oil). Alternately, you can place the jar in about an inch of simmering water and melt the oil in the same manner. Measure 3 tablespoons and add to the food processor with the remaining ingredients. Process the contents until very smooth.

Transfer the mixture to a container with a lid. Cover and refrigerate for a minimum of 6 hours to allow the flavors to blend. If desired, transfer the cheese to a decorative container and allow the cheese to soften for about 15 minutes at room temperature before serving.

Zesty Onion Dill Gournay

This savory, semi-soft cheese is bursting with onion and fresh dill flavor and makes a wonderful spread for crackers or crusty bread. The texture is similar to Boursin™, a trademarked brand of Gournay cheese. A food processor is recommended for efficient processing. This recipe yields about 8 oz.

Ingredients:

- ½ block (7 oz.) extra-firm water-packed tofu (do not use silken tofu)
- 3 T organic refined coconut oil
- 2 T fresh lemon juice
- 1 T prepared horseradish (not creamed)
- 2 tsp raw apple cider vinegar
- 1 tsp fine sea salt or kosher salt
- ½ tsp garlic powder
- ¼ tsp ground white pepper
- 2 T fresh minced dill
- 1 T dried minced onion

Technique:

Drain and press the tofu until it is not releasing any more liquid. (See Preparing Tofu for Recipes, pg. 10) Crumble the tofu into a food processor.

Remove the metal lid from the jar of coconut oil and place the jar in a microwave. Heat just until the solid oil liquefies, about 30 seconds to 1 minute (this will depend upon the solidity of the coconut oil). Alternately, you can place the jar in about an inch of simmering water and melt the oil in the same manner. Measure 3 tablespoons and add to the food processor with the remaining ingredients EXCEPT for the dill and dried onion. Process the contents until very smooth.

Transfer the mixture to a container with a lid and stir in the dill and dried onion. Cover and refrigerate for a minimum of 6 hours to allow the flavors to blend. If desired, transfer the cheese to a decorative container and allow the cheese to soften for about 15 minutes at room temperature before serving.

Miscellaneous Cheeses

Grated Parmesan

Grated Parmesan is very easy to make and can be substituted in any recipe that calls for grated dairy parmesan. Because this parmesan is made with miso, a fermented product or "living" food, the flavor will continue to develop during refrigeration. It will also stay fresh in the refrigerator for several weeks or more if stored in an airtight container.

Combine in a food processor:

- 1 cup almond meal*
- 1 T nutritional yeast
- 1 T mellow white miso paste
- ½ tsp sea salt or kosher salt
- ½ tsp onion powder
- ¼ tsp garlic powder

Process all ingredients until well blended and finely ground. Refrigerate in a covered container until ready to use.

*Bob's Red Mill™ produces an excellent almond meal. You can also grind blanched almonds in the food processor; just be sure to "pulse" in short bursts until finely ground, as continuous processing will turn the almonds into almond butter.

Tip: If you are allergic to soy, look for miso paste made from barley or chickpeas.

Garlic Parmesan Crostini

To prepare garlic parmesan crostini, slice a crusty loaf of Italian bread or French bread ¼-inch thick on the bias (diagonal).

Cut a clove of garlic in half and gently rub over each slice of bread.

Brush each slice with olive oil and place the slices in a single layer on a baking sheet. Sprinkle the slices with Grated Parmesan (see preceding recipe) and bake at 325°F until golden brown.

Basil Pesto

Pesto is a sauce originating in Genoa in the northern region of Italy. The name is derived from the Italian "pestare", which means to pound, or to crush, in reference to the original method of preparation with mortar and pestle. However, for the sake of convenience, pesto can be prepared in a food processor.

Ingredients:

- 5 cloves garlic
- ⅓ cup pine nuts or chopped walnuts
- 1 large bunch fresh basil leaves (about 2 cups)
- ⅓ cup olive oil
- ½ tsp coarse ground black pepper, or more to taste
- ¼ tsp sea salt or kosher salt, or more to taste
- ⅓ cup Grated Parmesan (pg. 89)

Technique:

Preheat the oven to 350°F. Place the garlic cloves on a baking sheet lined with foil and roast for 5 minutes. Remove the baking sheet from the oven and scatter the nuts in a single layer next to the garlic. Return to the oven and roast for 5 to 6 minutes until the nuts are lightly toasted; avoid over-browning. Remove from the oven and set aside to cool.

When cooled, add the garlic and nuts to a food processor and process until finely ground. Add the basil leaves, salt and pepper and process until puréed. While the processor is running, pour the olive oil into the mixture through the food chute and process for about 30 seconds. Stop the motor and add the parmesan. Process until combined. Add additional salt and pepper to taste as desired. The sauce will last in the refrigerator for about 1 week. Pesto does not require cooking before using in recipes.

Mascarpone

Non-dairy mascarpone is an uncultured, spreadable dessert cheese made from whole raw cashews. It resembles cream cheese although it tends to be slightly softer, with a pale cream color, light buttery flavor and a hint of natural sweetness.

Mascarpone is best known as an ingredient in the Italian dessert Tiramisu. Try it as a reduced-fat butter or margarine alternative for toast, bagels or muffins. A high-powered blender is required for efficient processing. This recipe yields about 12 oz.

Ingredients:

- 1 and ½ cup (7.5 oz. by weight) whole raw cashews
- ¼ cup organic refined coconut oil
- 2 T water
- 1 T fresh lemon juice
- 2 tsp raw apple cider vinegar
- ½ tsp sea salt or kosher salt

Technique:

Soak the nuts for a minimum of 8 hours in the refrigerator with enough water to cover. Drain the nuts, discarding the soaking water, and add them to a high-powered blender.

Remove the metal lid from the jar of coconut oil and place the jar in a microwave. Heat just until the solid oil liquefies, about 30 seconds to 1 minute (this will depend upon the solidity of the coconut oil). Alternately, you can place the jar in about an inch of simmering water and melt the oil in the same manner. Measure ¼ cup and add to the blender with the remaining ingredients.

Process the contents on high speed until completely smooth and creamy, stopping to scrape down the sides of the blender jar and push the mixture down into the blades as necessary (use a tamper tool if you have one). Transfer to a container with a lid and refrigerate until well-chilled and thickened.

Note: If you're preparing the mascarpone for Chocolate Mascarpone Cheesecake (pg. 137), there's no need to refrigerate and firm the mixture; proceed to use the mascarpone in the recipe immediately after blending.

Cheese Sauces

Golden Cheese Sauce

This velvety cheese sauce has a mild cheddar flavor that will please the entire family. It's ideal for making macaroni and cheese and cheesy rice. Or try pouring it over freshly steamed vegetables or baked potatoes. This recipe yields about 2 cups of sauce.

Ingredients:

- 1 and ¾ cup plain unsweetened soymilk with no additives
- 5 T tapioca flour
- ¼ cup vegetable oil
- ¼ cup nutritional yeast
- 1 T mellow white miso paste
- 1 tsp organic tomato paste (for a richer golden color, increase by one teaspoon)
- 1 tsp raw apple cider vinegar
- 1 tsp dry ground mustard
- ¾ tsp sea salt or kosher salt
- ½ tsp onion powder
- ¼ tsp ground white pepper

Technique:

Process the ingredients in a blender until smooth. Please note that the light golden color will develop as the cheese cooks. Transfer to a medium saucepan and cook the mixture over medium-low heat, stirring slowly and continually with a silicone/rubber spatula.

As the mixture begins to form curds, stir vigorously, scraping the sides and bottom of the saucepan with the spatula as you stir. Keep stirring until the mixture becomes bubbly, smooth and glossy. Taste and add salt as desired and/or additional soymilk to lighten the consistency to your preference. Reduce the heat to low to keep warm until ready to serve. Stir occasionally. The sauce will thicken upon cooling.

Classic Mac' and Cheese

An American classic; creamy, cheesy comfort food at its finest!

Ingredients for the macaroni:

- 2 cups elbow macaroni
- salted water
- 2 cups Golden Cheese Sauce (pg. 92)

Technique:

Prepare the macaroni according to package directions and cook until desired tenderness. While the macaroni is cooking, prepare the cheese sauce and keep warm over low heat, stirring occasionally.

Pour the macaroni from the cooking pot into a colander and shake to remove as much water as possible. Add the macaroni back to the warm cooking pot and toss thoroughly. The residual heat of the cooking pot will help evaporate any remaining water – this is very important or the water will dilute the cheese sauce! Stir in the cheese sauce.

At this point, you can transfer to a serving dish and serve immediately, or transfer the macaroni and cheese to a lightly oiled 8-inch baking dish and top with 2 tablespoons of fine dry breadcrumbs tossed with 2 teaspoons melted Better Butter (pg. 12). Broil for about 3 to 4 minutes or until golden brown on top; serve immediately.

Scalloped Potatoes Gratin

Sliced potatoes are baked in a luscious cheese sauce until tender and delicious!

Ingredients:

- 2 pounds russet potatoes (about 4 potatoes)
- Better Butter (pg. 12)
- 2 cups Golden Cheese Sauce (pg. 92)
- ½ tsp dried thyme
- sea salt or kosher salt and coarse ground black pepper

Technique:

Peel and thinly slice your potatoes (about ⅛-inch thick). A mandoline works great for this, but watch your fingers! Place the slices in water so they do not oxidize (turn brown).

Preheat the oven to 375°F. Prepare the cheese sauce and keep warm over low heat, stirring occasionally.

Next, "butter" a casserole dish with the butter. Drain the potatoes and pat them dry. Place a layer of potato slices in an overlapping pattern and season with salt and pepper. Spoon a little of the cheese sauce over the potatoes and spread evenly.

Continue to layer the potatoes with a sprinkle of salt and pepper and the cheese mixture. Sprinkle the top with the dried thyme and bake uncovered for 45 minutes. Set the oven on "broil" and cook an additional 5 minutes or until top begins to brown. Serve immediately.

Sauce Fromage Blanc

This smooth, mild and creamy white cheese sauce is perfect for pouring over pasta, potatoes, vegetables or savory filled crêpes. This recipe yields about 2 cups of sauce.

Ingredients:

- 1 and ¾ cup plain unsweetened soymilk with no additives (see pg. 8)
- ¼ cup vegetable oil
- ¼ cup (4 T) tapioca flour
- 2 T nutritional yeast
- 2 T dry sherry or dry white wine
- 1 T sesame tahini
- 1 tsp sea salt or kosher salt
- 1 tsp dry ground mustard
- pinch of freshly grated nutmeg

Technique:

Process the ingredients in a blender until smooth. Transfer to a medium saucepan and cook the mixture over medium-low heat, stirring slowly and continually with a silicone/rubber spatula.

As the mixture begins to form curds, stir vigorously, scraping the sides and bottom of the saucepan with the spatula as you stir. Keep stirring until the mixture becomes bubbly, smooth and glossy. Taste and add salt as desired and/or additional soymilk to lighten the consistency to your preference. Reduce the heat to low to keep warm until ready to serve. Stir occasionally. The sauce will thicken upon cooling.

Hot Jack-Crab and Cheese Dip

Shredded green jackfruit is combined with sautéed onion, Sauce Fromage Blanc and seasonings. The mixture is then baked to perfection and served with warm crostini for dipping.

Canned green jackfruit is used in this recipe to add amazing texture. It has no real flavor of its own and no protein value, but it has an uncanny resemblance to crab meat when shredded. It can be found in Indian and Asian markets. Look for the label "Green Jackfruit" or "Young Green Jackfruit" and be sure that it's packed in water or brine, not syrup. You may notice cans of ripe jackfruit stocked nearby but don't be tempted to substitute as it is very sweet when ripe and often packed in sugar syrup.

Ingredients:

- 1 can (about 20 oz.) green jackfruit in water or brine
- 2 T vegetable oil
- 1 medium onion, thinly sliced and then diced
- 1 T minced garlic (3 cloves)
- 2 cups (1 recipe) Sauce Fromage Blanc (pg. 95)
- 2 T chopped fresh parsley (or 2 tsp dry)
- 1 and ½ tsp Old Bay™ or Chesapeake Bay™ seasoning
- ½ tsp red pepper sauce, or more to taste
- sea salt or kosher salt and coarse ground black pepper, to taste
- optional: Garlic Parmesan Crostini for dipping (pg. 89)

Technique:

Drain the liquid from the can of jackfruit. Rinse the fruit thoroughly (especially if it was packed in brine) and drain in a colander. With a sharp knife, remove the tough core from each chunk of jackfruit and discard. Break the chunks apart with your fingers and remove the soft seeds and discard.

Wrap the stringy pulp in a paper towel or clean kitchen towel and squeeze to remove any excess remaining water. Add the chunks of jackfruit to a food processor and pulse a few times to shred into flakes. Do not purée the fruit. Set aside. Preheat the oven to 350°F.

In a non-stick skillet, heat the vegetable oil over medium heat and sauté the onion until translucent. Add the garlic and shredded jackfruit and sauté an additional 2 minutes. Transfer to a mixing bowl.

Prepare the cheese sauce and pour over the shredded jackfruit mixture in the mixing bowl. Add the parsley, seasoning and pepper sauce and salt and black pepper to taste; mix thoroughly. Transfer the mixture to a well-oiled casserole dish and bake for 30 minutes or until bubbly. Serve with warm bread, crackers or Garlic Parmesan Crostini for dipping.

Roasted Asparagus Crêpes
with Sauce Fromage Blanc

Asparagus spears are roasted until tender crisp, wrapped in tender crêpes and then topped with a velvety white cheese sauce. A crêpe is a type of very thin pancake. Since eggs are the primary ingredient of crêpes, creating eggless crêpes proved to be a bit of a challenge. Eggless crêpes will not brown quite as well and will have a slightly heavier texture than egg crêpes, but the combination of ingredients in this recipe will produce 8 very thin, tender and light golden crêpes that work well with this dish. You will need a crêpe pan or a non-stick skillet with sloping sides. It is very helpful to have a flexible spatula for lifting the edges of the crêpes and for flipping them over.

Ingredients for the crêpes:

- 1 and ¼ cup all-purpose flour
- 1 T organic sugar
- 1 tsp baking powder
- ½ tsp sea salt
- 1 and ¾ cup plain non-dairy milk
- 2 T Better Butter (pg. 12), melted
- vegetable oil to grease the crêpe pan or skillet
- Sauce Fromage Blanc (pg. 95)

For the roasted asparagus, you will need:

- 1 large bunch asparagus spears, preferably thin
- olive oil
- sea salt or kosher salt and coarse ground black pepper

Technique:

Prepare the asparagus by trimming off any woody ends. For thicker stalks, use a potato peeler to remove some of the tough, fibrous exterior near the bottom of the spears. Set aside.

Sift together the flour, sugar, baking powder and salt into a large mixing bowl. Pour in the milk and add the butter or margarine. Whisk until a smooth, thin batter is achieved. Let the batter sit for 15 minutes, whisking occasionally; this will ensure that the flour has absorbed the milk and the sugar has completely dissolved.

While the batter is sitting, preheat the oven to 425°F.

Now, heat the crêpe pan or non-stick skillet over medium heat for a minimum of 5 minutes. It is essential that the pan is hot.

Pour about 1 tablespoon of oil into the pan and with a crumpled paper towel, wipe the skillet, removing the excess oil. Have a bowl nearby to place the oily towel. You will need to re-wipe the skillet with the oily towel for each crêpe.

Have your bowl of batter near the stove and with a ⅓-cup measuring cup, ladle up the batter. Remove the pan from the heat and hold near the bowl of batter. Pour the batter into the center of the pan and quickly tilt the pan to the side and rotate in a circular motion to spread the batter in a thin layer. Place back over the heat.

When the surface of the crêpe appears dry, use the tip of the spatula to gently loosen it around the edges.

The edges of the crêpe will have curled up slightly, so carefully lift the edge of the crêpe with your fingers to check the color (you can also do this with the spatula if you prefer).

When the bottom-side of the crêpe appears to have a pale golden color, use the spatula to carefully flip the crêpe over. Cook for an additional minute.

When done, slide the crêpe onto a plate and cover with a piece of parchment paper or a kitchen towel to keep warm and moist. Repeat the process for the additional crêpes.

Next, place the asparagus in a single layer on a cookie sheet. Drizzle generously with a good quality olive oil, toss to coat and season with salt and pepper. Roast for exactly 18 minutes. Leave the oven on.

While the asparagus is roasting, prepare the cheese sauce and keep warm over low heat, stirring occasionally.

Now, place several roasted asparagus spears onto a crêpe and roll up, placing the crêpe seam side down in a lightly oiled baking dish. Repeat with the additional crêpes and asparagus spears. Place in the hot oven for 5 to 10 minutes to re-warm.

Transfer the crêpes to serving plates and top with a generous amount of cheese sauce. Garnish with additional black pepper and serve immediately.

Queso Nacho Sauce

As the name implies, this Mexican-style cheese sauce is perfect for topping nachos. This recipe yields about 2 cups of sauce.

Ingredients:

- 1 and ¾ cup plain unsweetened soymilk with no additives (see pg. 8)
- 5 T tapioca flour
- ¼ cup vegetable oil
- ¼ cup nutritional yeast
- 1 T mellow white miso paste
- 1 tsp ancho chili powder
- 1 tsp onion powder
- 1 tsp raw apple cider vinegar
- ¾ tsp sea salt or kosher salt
- ¼ tsp ground red pepper or cayenne pepper

Technique:

Process the ingredients in a blender until smooth. Please note that the golden color will develop as the cheese cooks. Transfer to a medium saucepan and cook the mixture over medium-low heat, stirring slowly and continually with a silicone/rubber spatula.

As the mixture begins to form curds, stir vigorously, scraping the sides and bottom of the saucepan with the spatula as you stir. Keep stirring until the mixture becomes bubbly, smooth and glossy. Taste and add salt as desired and/or additional soymilk to lighten the consistency to your preference. Reduce the heat to low to keep warm until ready to serve. Stir occasionally. The sauce will thicken upon cooling.

Tip: For a hot cheesy nacho bean dip, heat 1 can (16 oz.) vegetarian refried beans in a saucepan and stir in 1 cup queso nacho sauce. Garnish with pickled sliced jalapenos, diced onion and chopped cilantro, if desired.

Queso Blanco Sauce
(Mexican White Cheese Sauce)

This Mexican-style white cheese sauce is flavored with mild green chilies and is wonderful for dipping warm tortillas or tortilla chips or pouring over your favorite Mexican or Tex-Mex foods. This recipe yields about 2 cups of sauce.

Ingredients:

- 1 and ¾ cup plain unsweetened soymilk with no additives (see pg. 8)
- ¼ cup (4 T) tapioca flour
- ¼ cup vegetable oil
- 1 T nutritional yeast
- 2 tsp white wine vinegar
- 1 tsp ground cumin
- 1 tsp sea salt or kosher salt
- ½ tsp onion powder
- 1 can (4 oz.) diced mild green chilies
- 2 T finely minced onion
- garnish: 1 T chopped fresh cilantro (optional)

Technique:

Process the ingredients EXCEPT for the chilies, minced onion and cilantro in a blender until smooth. Transfer to a medium saucepan and add the chilies and minced onion. Cook the mixture over medium-low heat, stirring slowly and continually with a silicone/rubber spatula.

As the mixture begins to form curds, stir vigorously, scraping the sides and bottom of the saucepan with the spatula as you stir. Keep stirring until the mixture becomes bubbly, smooth and glossy. Taste and add salt as desired and/or additional soymilk to lighten the consistency to your preference. Reduce the heat to low to keep warm until ready to serve. Stir occasionally. The sauce will thicken upon cooling. Garnish with the optional cilantro before serving if desired.

Chik'n Enchiladas Suizas

Tender shreds of vegan chicken are bathed in a zesty Mexican white cheese sauce, wrapped in flour tortillas and then baked with a topping of additional cheese sauce and green enchilada sauce.

Ingredients:

- 20 oz. vegan chicken
- 1 T vegetable oil
- 2 cups Queso Blanco Sauce (pg. 100)
- 8 soft taco/enchilada-size flour tortillas (or flour/corn flour blend)
- 1 can (19 oz.) green chili enchilada sauce
- garnishes of your choice: Sour Cream (pg. 28), chopped cilantro, avocado slices, diced tomato or salsa and/or sliced black olives

Technique:

In a skillet over medium heat, add 1 tablespoon of oil and sauté the vegan chicken until lightly golden on both sides. Remove the chik'n and set aside to cool.

Once cooled, tear the chik'n into shreds and then coarsely chop with a knife. Place the shreds in a mixing bowl and set aside.

Prepare the queso blanco sauce and pour 1 and ½ cup of the sauce into the mixing bowl. Stir until all the chik'n and cheese sauce are combined.

Preheat the oven to 350°F and grease a large, shallow baking dish with vegetable oil.

Place a flour tortilla on your work surface and spoon about ½ cup of the filling along the edge. Roll up from the filling side, and place seam side down in the oiled dish. Repeat the process with the remaining tortillas and filling.

Top the enchiladas with the remaining ½ cup queso blanco sauce and follow with the green enchilada sauce (it may appear that there is an excess of sauce but the enchiladas will absorb a substantial amount when baked).

Cover the dish with foil and bake 30 minutes. Remove the foil and continue baking 10 minutes or until thoroughly heated. Garnish individual servings with toppings of your choice.

Salsa con Queso

Zesty and cheesy Salsa con Queso is wonderful served as a dip with tortilla chips or warm tortillas. It can also be used as a topping for your favorite Mexican and Tex-Mex dishes. This recipe yields about 2 cups of sauce.

Ingredients:

- ¾ cup plain unsweetened soymilk with no additives (see pg. 8)
- ¼ cup nutritional yeast
- ¼ cup (4 T) tapioca flour
- ¼ cup vegetable oil
- 1 tsp onion powder
- ½ tsp sea salt or kosher salt
- ½ tsp garlic powder
- ¼ tsp ancho chili powder
- 1 cup red tomato salsa of your choice

Technique:

Place all ingredients EXCEPT for the salsa in a blender and process until smooth. Please note that the golden color will develop as the cheese cooks. Transfer to a medium saucepan, add the salsa and cook the mixture over medium-low heat, stirring slowly and continually with a silicone/rubber spatula.

As the mixture begins to form curds, stir vigorously, scraping the sides and bottom of the saucepan with the spatula as you stir. Keep stirring until the mixture becomes thickened, bubbly and glossy. Taste and add salt as desired and/or additional soymilk to lighten the consistency to your preference. Reduce the heat to low to keep warm until ready to serve or keep warm in a mini crock pot or heated chafing dish. Stir occasionally.

Cheese Melts

As the name implies, cheese melts have the consistency of, well... melted cheese. They're thicker than cheese sauces which make them ideal for spreading on sandwiches before grilling or for stirring into any recipe where a uniformly melted cheese is desired, such as mashed potatoes, casseroles or cheesy soups (uniform melting is a common problem with many commercial non-dairy cheeses).

Cheese melts are very easy and economical to make too, and since they are intended to have a melted consistency, they require no gelling agents such as agar or carrageenan. A small amount of guar gum or xanthan gum is added for viscosity and to give the cheese stretch. They can be prepared and used immediately in recipes or refrigerated for later use, which makes them very convenient.

Any unused portions should be refrigerated in a food storage container with a lid. They can then be spread directly on sandwich breads before grilling or stirred into hot foods (when chilled, the cheese melts become very thick and sticky but will re-melt instantly when heated). They can also be gently reheated in a small saucepan or in the microwave when ready to use. There are four cheese melts offered: Colby (pg. 104), Jarlsberg (pg. 106), Tangy Cheddar (pg. 107) and Gruyère (pg. 109), with each recipe yielding about 1 cup of melted cheese.

For questions and advice regarding the recipes,
please join the Gentle Chef Group on Facebook:
https://www.facebook.com/groups/thegentlechef

To view the full-color photo gallery of the recipes in this book,
please visit The Gentle Chef website at: http://thegentlechef.com

Colby Melt

Colby is a mellow, golden cheese which can best be described as having a mild cheddar flavor. This cheese makes the perfect melt for Classic Grilled Cheese sandwiches (pg. 108). It's also wonderful for topping nachos. This recipe yields about 1 cup of melted cheese.

Ingredients:

- ¾ cup plain unsweetened soymilk with no additives (see pg. 8)
- ¼ cup vegetable oil
- 3 T tapioca flour
- 2 T nutritional yeast
- 1 T mellow white miso paste
- 1 T organic tomato paste
- ½ tsp onion powder
- ½ tsp dry ground mustard
- ¼ tsp sea salt or kosher salt
- ¼ tsp xanthan gum or guar gum

Technique:

Add the ingredients to a mini or standard blender and process the contents until smooth. Transfer to a small saucepan and cook the mixture over medium-low heat, stirring slowly and continually with a silicone/rubber spatula. The golden color will develop as the mixture cooks.

Increase stirring speed as the mixture thickens and begins to form curds. Stir vigorously until the mixture becomes very thick, smooth and glossy. For a more fluid consistency, keep warm over low heat, stirring occasionally, until ready to use in your recipe. For a spreadable consistency, remove from the heat and allow the melt to thicken.

Twice-Baked Cheesy Broccoli Potatoes

Baked potato shells are stuffed with a blend of mashed potato, broccoli and melted cheese and re-baked until golden brown on top. This recipe serves 2 to 4.

Ingredients:

- 2 extra-large russet potatoes
- 1 and ½ cup chopped broccoli florets (or try cauliflower)
- 1 cup Colby Melt (pg. 104) or Tangy Cheddar Melt (pg. 107)
- sea salt or kosher salt and coarse ground black pepper to taste

Technique:

Preheat the oven to 400°F. Thoroughly scrub and rinse the potatoes under running water. Blot dry. Deeply pierce the potatoes twice on each side. Rub the potatoes with a scant amount of vegetable oil and place them directly on a middle oven rack. Bake for 1 hour.

Remove the potatoes and let them cool until they can be handled comfortably without burning your hands. Reduce the oven heat to 350°F. While the potatoes are cooling, prepare the cheese melt and keep warm over low heat.

Lightly steam the broccoli florets, about 1 minute. For a quick and easy way to do this if you prefer, place the florets in a microwave-safe bowl, cover with a dampened paper towel and microwave for 1 minute.

Slice the potatoes in half lengthwise and scoop out the pulp into a mixing bowl. Be sure to leave a little bit of the potato around the shell for support. Mash the potato pulp with a potato masher or ricer. Add the cheese Melt and stir thoroughly. Fold in the broccoli florets and season with salt and pepper to taste. Stuff the potato halves with the potato mixture and place them on a baking sheet. Bake the stuffed potatoes for 30 minutes and then place them under the broiler for about 3 to 5 minutes until golden brown on top. Serve immediately.

Jarlsberg Melt

Jarlsberg shares flavor similarities with Swiss cheese and can best be described as mild, buttery and nutty with a hint of sweetness. This cheese also makes a wonderful melt for Classic Grilled Cheese sandwiches (pg. 108). This recipe yields about 1 cup of melted cheese.

Ingredients:

- ¾ cup plain unsweetened soymilk with no additives (see pg. 8)
- ¼ cup vegetable oil
- 3 T tapioca flour
- 2 T nutritional yeast
- 2 T dry white wine
- 1 T sesame tahini
- ½ tsp sea salt or kosher salt
- ¼ tsp dry ground mustard
- ¼ tsp xanthan gum or guar gum

Technique:

Add the ingredients to a mini or standard blender and process the contents until smooth. Transfer to a small saucepan and cook the mixture over medium-low heat, stirring slowly and continually with a silicone/rubber spatula.

Increase stirring speed as the mixture thickens and begins to form curds. Stir vigorously until the mixture becomes very thick, smooth and glossy. For a more fluid consistency, keep warm over low heat, stirring occasionally, until ready to use in your recipe. For a spreadable consistency, remove from the heat and allow the melt to thicken.

Tangy Cheddar Melt

Tangy Cheddar Melt has a sharp bite which makes it a lively alternative to the milder Colby. This recipe yields about 1 cup of melted cheese.

Ingredients:

- ¾ cup plain unsweetened soymilk with no additives (see pg. 8)
- ¼ cup vegetable oil
- 3 T tapioca flour
- 2 T nutritional yeast
- 2 T mellow white miso paste
- 2 tsp fresh lemon juice
- 1 tsp raw apple cider vinegar
- 1 tsp tomato paste*
- ½ tsp onion powder
- ¼ tsp dry ground mustard
- ¼ tsp xanthan gum or guar gum

*For tangy white cheddar, simply omit the tomato paste.

Technique:

Add the ingredients to a mini or standard blender and process the contents until smooth. Transfer to a small saucepan and cook the mixture over medium-low heat, stirring slowly and continually with a silicone/rubber spatula. The light golden color will develop as the mixture cooks.

Increase stirring speed as the mixture thickens and begins to form curds. Stir vigorously until the mixture becomes very thick, smooth and glossy. For a more fluid consistency, keep warm over low heat, stirring occasionally, until ready to use in your recipe. For a spreadable consistency, remove from the heat and allow the melt to thicken.

Classic Grilled Cheese

Cheese Melts are ideal for making grilled cheese sandwiches. If desired, other fillings can be added such as vegan deli slices, vegan bacon, sliced tomato and/or avocado slices. The Cheese Melt recipes will make about 1 cup of melted cheese which should be enough for 3 to 4 sandwiches.

For the sandwiches you will need:

- Cheese Melt of your choice (see pg. 103)
- Better Butter (pg. 12), room temperature
- sliced bread of your choice
- additional fillings of your choice

Technique:

Butter one side of all the bread slices. Spread the cheese on the non-buttered side of half of the bread slices. Layer with any additional fillings and top with the remaining slices of bread, butter side out. Place the sandwiches in a skillet over medium heat. Grill until golden brown on each side. Slice in half and serve.

Gruyère Melt

Gruyère cheese has a nutty and slightly salty flavor with a unique ripened quality without being acidic. While this complex flavor is difficult to imitate, this melt captures the flavor of melted Gruyère fairly well, while retaining its own unique character.

Gruyère Melt is ideal for spreading on crusty bread to top French Onion Soup (pg. 110) before placing under the broiler. Stir Gruyère Melt into mashed potatoes to add flavor and creaminess. (See Gruyère and Chive Mashed Potatoes, pg. 111) This recipe yields about 1 cup of melted cheese.

Ingredients:

- ¾ cup plain unsweetened soymilk with no additives (see pg. 8)
- ¼ cup vegetable oil
- 3 T tapioca flour
- 1 T nutritional yeast
- 2 T mellow white miso paste
- 1 T dry sherry
- 1 T sesame tahini
- ½ tsp onion powder
- ½ tsp dry ground mustard
- ¼ tsp sea salt or kosher salt
- ¼ tsp xanthan gum or guar gum

Technique:

Add all of the ingredients to a mini or standard blender and process the contents until smooth. Transfer to a small saucepan and cook the mixture over medium-low heat, stirring slowly and continually with a silicone/rubber spatula.

Increase stirring speed as the mixture thickens and begins to form curds. Stir vigorously until the mixture becomes very thick, smooth and glossy. For a more fluid consistency, keep warm over low heat, stirring occasionally, until ready to use in your recipe. For a spreadable consistency, remove from the heat and allow the melt to thicken.

French Onion Soup

A classic soup comprised of tender caramelized onions simmered in a savory brown vegetable broth, topped with crusty bread and melted Gruyère and then broiled until the cheese is lightly browned and bubbly.

Ingredients:

- ¼ cup (4 T) Better Butter (pg. 12) or olive oil
- 3 large sweet yellow onions, thinly sliced
- 2 tsp organic sugar
- 1 T all-purpose flour
- 5 and ¾ cups vegan no-beef broth
- ¼ cup dry sherry or dry red wine
- 1 bay leaf
- 1 sprig fresh thyme
- 1 French baguette
- Gruyère Melt (pg. 109)

Technique:

Add the butter or oil to a large soup pot and place over medium heat. Stir in the sugar. Add the onions and sauté until caramelized.

Whisk in the flour until well blended with the onions. Slowly add the broth while stirring and bring to a boil. Stir in the dry sherry or wine and add the bay leaf and thyme. Reduce heat to a simmer, cover and cook for 30 minutes.

Preheat the oven to 325°F.

While the soup is simmering, prepare the Gruyère Melt. After preparation, remove from the heat to allow the melt to thicken.

Cut 1-inch thick slices of bread. Place the slices on a baking sheet and toast until lightly browned and crisp, about 10 minutes. Remove from the oven. Set the oven on "Broil".

Remove the bay leaf and thyme stem and ladle the soup into oven-safe soup bowls. Spread a generous amount of the Gruyère melt on each bread slice and top each soup bowl. Place the soup bowls on the baking sheet for easier handling.

Place under the broiler just until the cheese is lightly browned and bubbly. Serve immediately.

Gruyère and Chive Mashed Potatoes
with Peppered Walnuts

Creamy mashed potatoes are blended with melted Gruyère cheese and fresh snipped chives and then garnished with peppery toasted walnuts.

Ingredients:

- 3 pounds Yukon Gold or russet potatoes, peeled and cut into 1-inch chunks
- 1 T olive oil
- 1 cup raw walnut pieces
- sea salt or kosher salt and coarse ground black pepper
- 1 cup Gruyère Melt (pg. 109)
- plain unsweetened non-dairy milk
- 2 T snipped fresh chives

Technique:

Preheat the oven to 350°F. Toss the walnuts in a bowl with the olive oil and a generous amount of pepper. Scatter on a baking sheet and roast for 10 minutes. Remove and set aside.

Place the potatoes in a large pot and cover completely with water. Stir in 2 tsp salt and bring to a boil. Cook the potatoes until tender, about 15 to 20 minutes.

While the potatoes are cooking, prepare the Gruyère Melt. Set aside on low heat to keep warm.

Drain the potatoes and transfer to a large mixing bowl. Mash the potatoes with a potato masher or ricer until crumbly. Add the Gruyère Melt and ¼ cup non-dairy milk and season with salt and pepper to taste. Whip the potatoes with an electric beater until smooth. Add additional milk as needed until a smooth and creamy but fluffy consistency is achieved. Stir in the snipped chives. Serve immediately and garnish with the peppered walnuts.

Elegant Swiss Fondue

Fondue is a Swiss and French dish of melted cheese served in a communal pot (caquelon) over a portable stove (réchaud) and eaten by dipping long-stemmed forks with bread and/or vegetables into the cheese. The fondue can also be kept warm in a commercial fondue pot or small crock pot.

The cheese fondue mixture should be kept warm enough to keep the fondue smooth and liquid but not so hot that it burns. If this temperature is held until the fondue is finished there will be a thin layer of toasted (not burnt) cheese at the bottom of the fondue pot. This is called "la religieuse" (French for "the nun") and is considered a treat. This recipe yields 4 cups or 1 quart of elegant Swiss fondue. For a half portion (2 cups), simply divide the recipe measurements in half.

Ingredients:

- 3 cups plain unsweetened soymilk with no additives (see pg. 8)
- ½ cup plus 2 T tapioca flour
- ½ cup vegetable oil
- ¼ cup nutritional yeast
- ¼ cup dry sherry or dry white wine
- 2 T sesame tahini
- 2 T mellow white miso paste
- 1 and ½ tsp sea salt or kosher salt, or more to taste
- 1 tsp onion powder
- 1 tsp dry ground mustard
- ½ tsp ground white pepper
- pinch of paprika
- pinch of fresh grated nutmeg
- 2 crushed cloves of garlic to rub the interior of the fondue or crock pot

Technique:

Rub the interior of the fondue or crock pot with the crushed garlic and discard.

In a blender, combine the fondue ingredients and process on low speed until smooth. Transfer to a large saucepan and cook the mixture over medium-low heat, stirring slowly and continually with a silicone/rubber spatula.

Increase stirring speed as the mixture thickens and begins to form curds. Stir vigorously until the mixture becomes very thick, smooth and glossy. Turn the heat to low to keep the fondue warm while you heat up the fondue or crock pot.

Taste and add salt as desired and/or additional soymilk to lighten the consistency to your preference, then transfer the mixture to the heated pot and serve with chunks of bread and raw or cooked vegetables. Stir the fondue occasionally to prevent the oil from separating and floating to the top of the fondue pot.

Tip: Make a figure 8 while dipping, as this will ensure that the cheese mixture is frequently stirred.

Eggless Eggs

Good Morning Scramble

The Good Morning Scramble is a basic tofu scramble. Try adding sautéed vegetables or top with one of the shredded cheeses from this cookbook. For a traditional American breakfast, serve with hash browns, vegan bacon or sausages and whole grain toast.

- 1 block (14 oz.) soft to firm water-packed tofu (silken tofu is not recommended for this recipe)
- 1 T nutritional yeast
- ½ tsp onion powder
- ¼ tsp kala namak (Himalayan black salt)
- ⅛ tsp paprika (a pinch)
- ⅛ tsp turmeric (a pinch)
- 2 T Better Butter (pg. 12)
- sea salt or kosher salt and coarse ground black pepper to taste

Drain and press the tofu until it is not releasing any more liquid. (See Preparing Tofu for Recipes, pg. 10)

In a mixing bowl, combine the nutritional yeast, onion powder, kala namak, paprika and turmeric. Crumble the tofu into the mixing bowl and toss thoroughly to coat with the seasoning.

Melt the butter in a skillet over medium heat. Do not let the butter brown. Add the seasoned tofu and "scramble" (push and fold the mixture with a spatula) until the tofu is heated through and resembles scrambled eggs. Season the scramble with salt and pepper to taste. Serve immediately.

Sunnyside-Ups

Delicate slices of silken tofu are lightly seasoned with kala namak (Himalayan black salt), gently pan-seared and then topped with no-yolks sauce. This rich sauce remarkably simulates egg yolk and is wonderful for dipping toast and vegan bacon or sausage.

Ingredients:

- 1 carton (12.3 oz.) extra-firm silken tofu
- kala namak (Himalayan black salt)
- vegetable oil spray
- No-Yolks Sauce (pg. 115)

Technique:

Cut open one end of the carton of silken tofu, drain the water and gently slide out the tofu. Handle it carefully as it is very delicate and will break easily. Place the tofu on a plate lined with several layers of paper towels or a clean lint-free kitchen towel to drain for a minimum of 20 minutes.

Transfer the tofu to a work surface, turn the block on its side and slice lengthwise with a sharp knife to create 4 slabs. If you're not concerned with creating rounds, slice each slab in half to make a total of 8 pieces about ¼-inch thick. To create rounds, use a 3-inch ring mold and cut each slab into a round, for a total of 4 rounds. Discard the remnants or save for another recipe.

Place a small amount of kala namak into a small dish and with a water-moistened fingertip carefully rub some of the salt over the tofu slices. Set aside.

Prepare the no-yolks sauce and keep warm over low heat, stirring occasionally, while continuing to the next step.

Mist a non-stick or well-seasoned cast iron skillet generously with vegetable oil spray and place over medium heat. When the skillet is hot, add the tofu slices and pan-sear until lightly golden on both sides. Transfer to a serving plate and spoon a generous teaspoon of the sauce onto the center of each slice. Pour additional sauce into individual serving cups on each plate for dipping.

No-Yolks Sauce

No-yolks sauce is a rich dipping sauce that remarkably simulates lightly-cooked liquid egg yolk.

Ingredients:

- ¼ cup Better Butter (pg. 12)
- 2 tsp unmodified potato starch, cornstarch or arrowroot powder
- 1 T nutritional yeast
- ¼ tsp kala namak (Himalayan black salt)
- ⅛ tsp paprika (a pinch)
- ⅛ tsp turmeric (a pinch)
- ½ cup water
- ¼ cup plain unsweetened soymilk with no additives

Technique:

In a small saucepan, melt the butter over low heat and whisk in the starch until smooth (do not let the butter brown).

Whisk in the nutritional yeast, kala namak, paprika and turmeric.

Whisk in the water and soymilk.

Increase the heat to medium-low and cook, stirring frequently until the sauce comes to a simmer. Immediately reduce the heat to low to keep warm and stir occasionally while you prepare the rest of your recipe.

Over-Easys

Delicately seasoned and crumbled silken tofu is lightly "scrambled" and served over whole grain English muffins or toast with a generous drizzle of no-yolks sauce. This dish is reminiscent of soft-boiled eggs served over toast.

Ingredients:

- 1 carton (12.3 oz.) extra-firm silken tofu
- ¼ tsp kala namak (Himalayan black salt)
- vegetable oil spray
- No-Yolks Sauce (pg. 115)
- 2 whole grain English Muffins or 2 slices of bread cut on the diagonal
- Better Butter (pg. 12), for buttering the toast or English muffins

Technique:

Cut open one end of the carton of silken tofu, drain the water and slide out the tofu. Slice the tofu into 4 slabs and place them on a plate lined with several layers of paper towels or a clean, lint-free kitchen towel to drain for a minimum of 20 minutes. Gently blot the tofu with additional towels to remove as much moisture as possible. This step is very important for the proper texture.

Prepare the no-yolks sauce and keep warm over low heat, stirring occasionally, while continuing to the next step.

Mist a non-stick or well-seasoned cast iron skillet generously with vegetable oil spray and place over medium heat. While the skillet is heating, toast the English muffins or bread slices.

When the skillet is hot, crumble the silken tofu into the skillet. Season with ¼ teaspoon of kala namak and gently "scramble" the tofu until lightly pan-seared and completely heated through. Remove from the heat. Butter the English muffins or toast and place on serving plates. Top with the scrambled silken tofu and generously drizzle with the no-yolks sauce. Garnish with black pepper and serve immediately.

Eggless Egg Omelettes

Light and delicate eggless egg omelettes can be filled with your choice of ingredients. For this omelette, I simply filled it with shredded block cheese and garnished with salsa. The cooking technique is very important with this recipe, so follow the directions carefully to ensure success. It is essential to use a non-stick skillet or well-seasoned cast iron skillet to prevent the omelettes from sticking. This recipe yields 2 omelettes.

Ingredients for the omelettes:

- 1 carton (12.3 oz.) extra-firm silken tofu
- 3 T cornstarch, unmodified potato starch or arrowroot flour
- 1 T nutritional yeast
- 1 T No-Eggy Mayo (pg. 133)
- ½ tsp onion powder
- ¼ tsp kala namak (Himalayan black salt)
- ⅛ tsp paprika or cayenne pepper (a pinch)
- ⅛ tsp turmeric (a pinch)
- fillings and toppings of your choice
- Better Butter (pg. 12)

Technique:

Cut open one end of the carton of silken tofu, drain the water and slide out the tofu. Slice the tofu into 4 slabs and place them on a plate lined with several layers of paper towels or a clean, lint-free kitchen towel to drain for a minimum of 20 minutes. Gently blot the tofu with additional towels to remove as much moisture as possible. This step is very important or the omelette will not set properly.

Crumble the tofu into a food processor and add the starch, nutritional yeast, mayonnaise, onion powder, kala namak, paprika or cayenne pepper and turmeric. Process the contents until smooth. The ingredients will form a thick, pale cream. Please note that the egg color will develop when the mixture is cooked. Transfer the mixture to a bowl and set aside while the filling is prepared.

If you will be using vegetables that have a high moisture content (e.g., mushrooms, spinach, zucchini, diced tomatoes), be sure to sauté them until they have released most of their liquid and are cooked through. Transfer the vegetables and other fillings to a separate bowl and set aside.

In the same non-stick skillet or well-seasoned cast iron skillet over medium heat, melt 2 tablespoons of butter. Add half (¾ cup) of the omelette mixture and spread evenly in the skillet with a rubber/silicone spatula or the back of a spoon. Cover the skillet with a lid. It doesn't matter if the lid was made for the skillet, or if it fits correctly, as long as the skillet can be covered to hold in steam while the omelette mixture cooks. Turn the heat down to just above low and let the mixture cook undisturbed. DO NOT STIR! The goal is to slow cook the omelette (the steam will help cook the surface).

Lift the lid to check the omelette after a few minutes. If the surface still appears wet, replace the lid and continue to cook until the surface is dry. This may take several minutes, so do not rush this step. Test the surface of the omelette with your finger, if it feels dry and somewhat firm to the touch, place the filling on one side of the omelette. With a wide spatula, carefully lift the opposite side of the omelette over the filling. Replace the lid and cook an additional 30 seconds or so to give the cheese a chance to melt.

Now slide the omelette onto a serving plate and place in a warm oven while you repeat the procedure with the second omelette. Be sure to add additional butter or margarine to the skillet before adding the omelette mixture.

Garnish with a dollop of Sour Cream (pg. 28), salsa or other toppings of choice, if desired.

Southwestern Scramble

Velvety eggless scramble, vegan sausage, onion, bell pepper and Pepper Jack cheese merge together in this favorite breakfast or brunch dish. This scramble will serve 4.

Ingredients:

- 1 block (14 oz.) soft to firm water-packed tofu (silken tofu is not recommended for this recipe)
- 1 T vegetable oil
- 10 oz. vegan sausage
- 1 T nutritional yeast
- ½ tsp onion powder
- ¼ tsp kala namak (Himalayan black salt)
- ⅛ tsp paprika (a pinch)
- ⅛ tsp turmeric (a pinch)
- 2 T Better Butter (pg. 12)
- 1 small onion, finely diced
- ½ bell pepper, finely diced
- sea salt or kosher salt and coarse ground black pepper to taste
- ½ cup shredded Pepper Jack cheese (pg. 63)
- salsa verde or red salsa

Technique:

Drain and press the tofu until it is not releasing any more liquid. (See Preparing Tofu for Recipes, pg. 10)

In a mixing bowl, combine the nutritional yeast, onion powder, kala namak, paprika and turmeric. Crumble the tofu into the mixing bowl and toss thoroughly to coat with the seasoning. Set aside.

Lightly coat a skillet with a little vegetable oil and brown the sausage over medium heat. Transfer to a separate bowl and set aside.

In the same skillet, sauté the onions and bell pepper in the butter or margarine over medium heat until tender. Add the tofu mixture and "scramble" (push and fold the mixture with a spatula) until the tofu is heated through and resembles scrambled eggs.

Add the sausage back to the skillet and stir to combine. Season the scramble with salt and pepper to taste. Top the contents of the skillet with the shredded Pepper Jack cheese. Cover, reduce heat to low and let "steam" until the cheese melts a bit. Serve and top with salsa of your choice.

No-No Huevos Rancheros

No-No Huevos Rancheros is my egg-free variation of Huevos Rancheros (Spanish for "rancher's eggs"). The basic dish consists of layers of homemade chunky salsa, refried beans and lightly fried corn tortillas. The layers are topped with pan-seared silken tofu with no-yolks sauce and garnished with sliced avocado and cilantro. Spanish rice is a suggested accompaniment.

There are several components to this dish but it's really very easy and the results are well worth the effort. This recipe yields 2 hearty servings.

Ingredients:

- 1 carton (12.3 oz.) extra-firm silken tofu
- 1 can (16 oz.) vegetarian or fat-free refried beans
- kala namak (Himalayan black salt)
- olive oil
- 4 corn tortillas
- sliced avocado
- optional: chopped cilantro for garnish
- No-Yolks Sauce (pg. 115)

Salsa Ingredients:

- olive oil
- ½ medium onion, chopped (about ½ cup)
- 1 can (15 oz.) diced tomatoes, preferably fire-roasted
  or 2 large vine-ripened tomatoes, when in season*
- 1 small can (4 oz.) diced green chilies
- 1 T minced garlic (3 cloves)
- 1 tsp ancho chili powder
  (or use ½ tsp ancho and ½ tsp chipotle for a spicier sauce)
- ½ tsp ground cumin
- sea salt or kosher salt to taste

*Fresh tomatoes should be blanched in boiling water for 1 minute to ease removal of the skins before dicing.

Technique:

Cut open one end of the carton of silken tofu, drain the water and gently slide out the tofu. Handle it carefully as it is very delicate and will break easily. Place the tofu on a plate lined with several layers of paper towels or a clean lint-free kitchen towel to drain for a minimum of 20 minutes.

Prepare the salsa (this can be done ahead of time, refrigerated and re-warmed prior to serving for convenience). Commercial chunky salsa can be substituted if desired.

To prepare the salsa, sauté the onions in 2 tablespoons of olive oil in a medium size skillet over medium heat. Once translucent, add the tomatoes and any juice from the tomatoes. If you are using fresh tomatoes, chop them first, then add. Please note that fresh tomatoes will take longer to cook than canned tomatoes, since canned tomatoes are already partially cooked during the canning process. Add the chopped green chilies and the seasonings. Bring to a simmer, reduce heat to low, and let simmer while you prepare the rest of the dish, stirring occasionally. Reduce heat to warm after the salsa has been simmering for 10 minutes (20 minutes for fresh tomatoes); add salt to taste.

Next, warm the refried beans in a covered saucepan over low heat. Add a little water as necessary to thin to a slightly saucy consistency.

Now, turn the tofu on its side and slice lengthwise with a sharp knife to create 4 slabs. If you wish to create rounds, use a 3-inch ring mold and cut each slab into a round, for a total of 4 rounds. Discard the remnants or save for a stir-fry.

Place a small amount of kala namak into a small dish and with a water-moistened fingertip carefully rub some of the salt over the tofu slices. Set aside.

Prepare the No-Yolks Sauce and keep warm over low heat, stirring occasionally, while you warm the tortillas and pan-sear the tofu slices.

Now prepare the tortillas. Heat the oven to its lowest setting and place serving plates in the oven to keep warm. Heat a tablespoon of olive oil in a large non-stick or well-seasoned cast iron skillet on medium high, coating the pan with the oil. One by one heat the tortillas in the skillet for a minute or two on each side until they are heated through and softened (add additional oil as necessary). Stack them on one of the warming plates in the oven to keep warm while the tofu is prepared.

Add another tablespoon of olive oil to the skillet and place over medium heat. When the skillet is hot, add the tofu slices and pan-sear until lightly golden on both sides.

To serve, spoon some of the salsa onto a warmed plate. Top with a tortilla, some refried beans and another tortilla. Place the tofu on top of the tortilla. Place a spoonful of no-yolks sauce in the center of the tofu and spoon the additional salsa around the tofu. Garnish with avocado slices and optional cilantro.

Garden Frittata

A frittata is essentially an open-faced omelette. Traditionally it is cooked on the stove and then placed under a broiler to set the top. However, my version is baked, which makes it a breeze to cook; and unlike omelettes which need to be prepared in a non-stick skillet or well-seasoned cast iron skillet, the frittata can be baked directly in a 9-inch oven-safe stainless steel skillet or aluminum pie plate. Chock full of colorful vegetables, the frittata makes a nice breakfast or brunch dish for 2.

Ingredients:

- 1 carton (12.3 oz.) extra-firm silken tofu
- 3 T unmodified potato starch, cornstarch or arrowroot powder
- 1 T nutritional yeast
- 1 T No-Eggy Mayo (pg. 133)
- ½ tsp onion powder
- ¼ tsp kala namak (Himalayan black salt)
- ¼ tsp coarse ground black pepper, or more to taste
- ⅛ tsp turmeric (a pinch)
- ⅛ tsp paprika or cayenne pepper (a pinch)
- 2 cups raw finely chopped or shredded vegetables of choice
- 2 T Better Butter (pg. 12) plus extra for "greasing" the skillet
- ½ tsp dried thyme
- optional: ½ cup shredded cheese that melts*

*See the chapter on Soymilk-Based Block Cheeses, pg. 49

Technique:

Cut open one end of the carton of silken tofu, drain the water and slide out the tofu. Slice the tofu into 4 slabs and place them on a plate lined with several layers of paper towels or a clean, lint-free kitchen towel to drain for a minimum of 20 minutes. Gently blot the tofu with additional towels to remove as much moisture as possible. This step is very important or the frittata will not set properly.

Crumble the tofu into a food processor and add the starch, nutritional yeast, mayonnaise, onion powder, kala namak, turmeric and paprika and process until smooth. The ingredients will form a thick, pale cream. Please note that the egg color will develop when the mixture is cooked. Transfer the mixture to a bowl and set aside while the vegetables are prepared.

Preheat the oven to 375°F. Generously grease a nine-inch oven-safe skillet (or pie plate) with butter or margarine and set aside.

Melt the butter or margarine in a separate skillet and sauté the vegetables until completely cooked through. This is especially important if using vegetables with a high moisture content (mushrooms and zucchini, for example). Transfer the vegetables to the bowl with the tofu mixture, add the thyme and stir thoroughly to combine.

Spoon the mixture into the oven skillet (or pie plate) and smooth the top with the spatula or back of a spoon. Top with the optional shredded cheese, if desired.

Bake for 35 minutes. Remove from the heat and let cool for about 10 minutes before slicing and serving. The frittata should also be fairly easy to remove from the skillet and placed on a serving plate. Simply slide a flat spatula underneath to loosen and remove.

French Toast

Sliced whole grain bread is dipped in an eggless egg mixture, pan-fried until golden brown and garnished with toppings of your choice.

You will need:

- 4 to 6 slices whole grain bread*
- vegetable oil
- toppings of your choice, such as real maple syrup, coconut syrup, fruit syrup or jam; or top with fruit compote and dust with organic powdered sugar

*Old bread is best (but not stale); or leave fresh bread out overnight exposed to the air. Whole grain bread has a heartier texture than white bread and is better for you too. There should be sufficient batter to make 6 slices of French toast.

And for the batter, process the following ingredients in a blender until smooth:

- ½ carton (6 oz.) extra-firm silken tofu
- ¾ cup plain unsweetened non-dairy milk
- 3 T unmodified potato starch, cornstarch or arrowroot flour
- 1 T nutritional yeast
- 1 T vegetable oil
- 1 T organic sugar, maple syrup or brown rice syrup
- 1 tsp real vanilla extract
- pinch of sea salt
- optional: ½ tsp cinnamon (or try pumpkin pie spice)

Technique:

Pour the blender ingredients into a pie plate or wide, shallow dish.

In a non-stick skillet or well-seasoned cast iron skillet over medium heat, add 2 tablespoons vegetable oil. Crumple a paper towel and wipe the oil around in the skillet (reserve the oily paper towel to re-wipe the skillet in between batches of French toast).

Dip a bread slice briefly into the batter. Coat both sides but do not soak. Gently slide the slice of bread between your fingers to remove the excess batter. Add the bread slice to the skillet and repeat with another slice. Fry until golden brown on each side. Test each piece in the center with the tip of the spatula or your finger to make sure the batter is cooked through and toast has firmed up. Set on a plate and place in a warm oven while you repeat the process with additional slices. Re-wipe the skillet with the oily paper towel as necessary before adding more battered bread.

Serve hot with a dab of Better Butter (pg. 12) and the toppings of your choice.

Eggless Eggs Florentine

This is my variation of a classic brunch favorite. Whole grain English muffins are layered with slices of crispy vegan bacon, silky seasoned tofu, tomato slices and sautéed spinach and then crowned with tarragon-infused Béarnaise sauce; serves 2 to 4.

Ingredients:

- 1 carton (about 12 oz.) extra-firm silken tofu
- kala namak (Himalayan black salt)
- Béarnaise Sauce (recipe follows)
- mild olive oil
- 8 slices vegan bacon
- 4 slices fresh tomato
- 8 oz. fresh spinach (or try mustard greens, kale or collard greens)
- 2 whole grain English muffins
- coarse ground black pepper to taste

Technique:

Cut open one end of the carton of silken tofu, drain the water and gently slide out the tofu. Handle it carefully as it is very delicate and will break easily. Place the tofu on a plate lined with several layers of paper towels or a clean lint-free kitchen towel to drain for a minimum of 20 minutes. Transfer the tofu to a work surface, turn the block on its side and slice lengthwise with a sharp knife to create 4 slabs. To create rounds, use a 3-inch ring mold and cut each slab into a round, for a total of 4 rounds. Discard the remnants or save for another recipe.

Place a small amount of kala namak into a small dish and with a water-moistened fingertip carefully rub some of the salt over the tofu slices. Set aside.

Next, prepare the Béarnaise sauce. For the sauce, you will need:

- 1 shallot, finely minced or 2 T minced red onion
- 2 tsp minced fresh tarragon or ¾ tsp dried
- 3 T dry white wine (e.g., Chardonnay, Sauvignon Blanc)
- 1 T white wine vinegar
- ¼ cup (4 T) Better Butter (pg. 12)
- 2 tsp unmodified potato starch, cornstarch or arrowroot powder
- ⅛ tsp turmeric (a pinch)
- ½ cup plain unsweetened soymilk with no additives
- ¼ cup water
- ¼ tsp sea salt or kosher salt
- ¼ tsp coarse ground black pepper

In a very small saucepan over medium-low heat, simmer the shallot (or red onion) and the tarragon in the wine and vinegar until the wine is reduced by half, about 5 minutes. Do not let the wine evaporate completely. Reduce the heat to low.

Add the butter or margarine and stir until melted. Whisk in the cornstarch and the turmeric.

Whisk in the milk and then the water. Increase the heat to medium-low and bring just to a simmer, stirring frequently. Add the salt and pepper.

Reduce the heat to low to keep warm until ready to serve. Stir occasionally.

Now, lightly coat a skillet with olive oil and place over medium-high heat. Cook the bacon until lightly browned and crisp around the edges – avoid overcooking or the bacon will be hard. Remove the slices and set aside.

Add the spinach to the same skillet and sauté until the moisture has been removed and the spinach is cooked through. Remove and set aside.

Add a little more vegetable oil to the skillet and over medium-high heat pan-sear the tofu slices on both sides until lightly golden. While the tofu is cooking, toast your English muffins.

To assemble: Place 2 slices of the bacon on each slice of the English muffins. Add a tomato slice on top of the bacon and top the tomato slice with the sautéed spinach. Top the spinach with a slice of tofu. Spoon the béarnaise sauce over the tofu and garnish with a sprinkle of black pepper. Serve immediately.

Mushroom, Onion and Swiss Quiche

Mushroom, Onion and Swiss Quiche is an open-faced pastry crust pie filled with a blend of silken tofu custard, shredded Alpine Swiss cheese and sautéed mushrooms and onions. Any combination of other vegetables or vegan "meats" can be substituted, as well as any of the firm soymilk-based cheeses in this book.

Ingredients:

- 2 cartons (12.3 oz. each) extra-firm silken tofu
- 1 basic pastry crust (recipe follows)
- 2 T vegetable oil
- ½ medium-size onion (about ½ cup)
- 6 oz. mushrooms, any variety, thinly sliced
- ⅓ cup unmodified potato starch, cornstarch or arrowroot powder
- 2 T nutritional yeast
- ¾ tsp kala namak (Himalayan black salt)
- ½ dried thyme
- ½ tsp coarse ground black pepper
- 1 cup shredded Alpine Swiss (pg. 74)

Notes: The mushrooms and onions can be substituted with any combination of vegetables or vegan "meats", however, avoid exceeding 10 ounces total (before cooking). It is essential to cook the ingredients thoroughly to remove as much moisture as possible in order for the quiche to set properly. Also, do not use cheeses other than the firm soymilk-based cheeses in this book. Commercial vegan cheeses are prepared differently and with different ingredients and may cause the quiche to not set properly.

Technique:

Cut open one end of each carton of silken tofu, drain the water and slide out the tofu. Slice each block into 4 slabs and place them on a plate lined with several layers of paper towels or a clean, lint-free kitchen towel to drain for a minimum of 20 minutes. Gently blot the tofu with additional towels to remove as much moisture as possible. This step is very important or the quiche will not set properly.

Prepare and pre-bake the pastry crust for 12 minutes at 375°F. Remove and let cool but leave the oven on.

Add the vegetable oil to a skillet and sauté the onions and mushrooms over medium heat until the mushrooms have completely released their moisture and the onions are beginning to caramelize. It is essential that the mixture be cooked thoroughly. Stir in the thyme and black pepper and set aside to cool.

Crumble the silken tofu into a food processor. Add the starch, yeast and kala namak. Process the contents until smooth. Transfer the tofu mixture to a mixing bowl. Stir in the sautéed mushrooms, onions and the shredded cheese. Mix thoroughly.

Spoon the filling into the pastry crust and smooth the surface with the back of the spoon. Bake uncovered for 55 minutes. Let the quiche cool for about 15 to 20 minutes to allow it to "set" before slicing and serving. If the quiche needs to be reheated, cover securely with foil and heat in the oven at 350°F for 10 to 15 minutes; or cover with plastic wrap and reheat in the microwave.

For the basic pastry crust, you will need:

Ingredients:

- 1 and ½ cup unbleached white wheat flour
- 1 tsp sea salt or kosher salt (for savory pies and quiches)
- ⅔ cup cold Better Butter (pg. 12)
- 3 T very cold water

Technique:

Measure the flour into a bowl and chill in the freezer for half an hour. Cut the butter or margarine into chunks, place in a bowl and likewise freeze for half an hour.

To make the dough in a food processor, combine the flour, salt, and butter in the processor and process until the mixture resembles coarse crumbs, about 10 seconds. With the machine running, add the cold water through the feed tube and pulse quickly 5 or 6 times, or until the dough comes together and starts to pull away from the sides of the container. Gather the dough into a ball, flatten it into a disk, and wrap in plastic wrap. Refrigerate for at least 1 hour.

To make the dough by hand, combine the flour, salt, and butter in a medium bowl, and mix with your fingertips until the mixture resembles coarse crumbs. Add the cold water 1 tablespoon at a time and mix until the dough comes together and is no longer dry, being careful not to over mix. Form into a disk, wrap in plastic wrap, and refrigerate for at least 1 hour.

With a rolling pin, roll the dough evenly on a lightly floured surface, about ⅛-inch thick. Place in a 9" pie plate and with a knife trim away any excess dough from the edge. Crimp the edges with a fork and then wrap in plastic; chill in the refrigerator until the filling is ready.

Bedeviled Eggless Eggs

Bedeviled eggless eggs are remarkably similar to deviled eggs in appearance, taste and texture. They make the perfect bite-size finger food for vegan BBQs, picnics and parties. Kala namak, or Himalayan black salt, is essential to impart that familiar egg-like taste to these savory bites. This recipe yields 16 to 24 bedeviled eggless eggs.

A blender is required for preparing the "egg whites" and a food processor is recommended for the "yolk filling". You will also need an 8" square baking pan and 1 block (14 oz.) of extra-firm water-packed tofu. Drain and press the tofu until it is not releasing any more liquid - this is very important! (See Preparing Tofu for Recipes, pg. 10) After pressing you will have approximately 12 oz. of tofu.

Ingredients for the "egg whites":

- ⅓ block of pressed tofu (about 4 oz.)
- ¾ tsp kala namak (Himalayan black salt)
- 2 cups water
- 1 T agar powder

Ingredients for the "yolk" filling:

- ⅔ block of pressed tofu (about 8 oz.)
- 3 T No-Eggy Mayo (pg. 133)
- 1 T nutritional yeast
- 1 T dill pickle brine
- 2 tsp Dijon mustard or spicy golden mustard
- ½ tsp onion powder
- ¼ tsp kala namak* (Himalayan black salt), or more to taste
- ¼ tsp turmeric
- ¼ tsp paprika (for extra bedeviling, use cayenne pepper)

Garnishes:

- paprika and coarse ground black pepper
- optional: sliced black olives; fresh snipped chives; capers or chopped dill

Technique:

To prepare the "egg whites", place the "egg white" ingredients into a blender and process until smooth. Pour the mixture into a saucepan and bring to rapid simmer over medium heat, stirring frequently to avoid scorching the tofu mixture. Pour the mixture into the 8" baking pan and set aside to cool.

Next, crumble the ⅔ block of tofu into the food processor and add the remaining "yolk" filling ingredients. Process the contents until completely smooth, stopping as necessary to scrape down the sides of the food processor. Alternately, the mixture can be mashed using a fork but the mixture will not be as smooth.

Transfer the "yolk" mixture to a bowl or food storage container, season with additional kala namak if desired, cover and refrigerate until ready to use. Cover the baking pan with plastic wrap or foil and refrigerate until the "egg whites" have completely set, or a minimum of 30 minutes.

Now, run a table knife around the perimeter of the baking pan to loosen the "egg white" (or simply pop them out of the chocolate "egg" molds). Invert the baking pan onto a clean work surface. At this point, the "egg white" can be cut into rectangles or cut into rounds or ovals.

For rectangles, cut the "egg whites" into 6 even strips. Turn your cutting surface and make 4 even slices. This will create 24 rectangles. For rounds or ovals, use a 1 and ½-inch to 1 and ¾-inch cookie cutter or ring mold. Any "egg white" remnants can be finely diced and mixed with any of the leftover "yolk" filling for a quick eggless salad sandwich.

Chef's note: I use a 1 and ¾-inch aluminum cookie cutter with a scalloped edge that was slightly pinched to create an oval, which is perfect for creating "egg" shapes with scalloped edges.

Spoon a generous teaspoonful of the "yolk" mixture onto the top of each "egg white". Alternately, the mixture can be decoratively piped onto the "egg whites" using a pastry bag. If you don't have a pastry bag, try placing the mixture into a zip-lock bag, seal and then snip off a tiny piece of the bottom corner of the bag with scissors. Squeeze the bag to pipe the mixture onto the "egg whites".

Sprinkle with paprika and garnish with optional ingredients as desired. Cover with plastic wrap and chill thoroughly before serving.

Eggless Egg Salad

This tasty sandwich filling remarkably resembles real egg salad in appearance taste and texture, but without the cholesterol (or animal cruelty). A blender is required for preparing the "egg whites" and a food processor is recommended for the "yolk" mixture. You will also need 1 block (14 oz.) of extra-firm water-packed tofu. Drain and press the tofu until it is not releasing any more liquid - this is very important! (See Preparing Tofu for Recipes, pg. 10) After pressing you will have approximately 12 oz. of tofu.

Ingredients for the "egg whites":

- ⅓ pressed block of tofu (about 4 oz.)
- ¾ tsp kala namak (Himalayan black salt)
- 2 cups water
- 1 T agar powder

Ingredients for the "yolk" mixture:

- ⅔ pressed block of tofu (about 8 oz.)
- ¼ cup No-Eggy Mayo (pg. 133) plus additional as necessary for consistency
- 1 T nutritional yeast
- 2 tsp prepared mustard, your choice of Dijon, spicy, golden or yellow
- ¼ tsp kala namak (Himalayan black salt), or more to taste
- ¼ tsp turmeric
- ¼ tsp paprika
- 2 T minced onion
- 1 rib of celery, diced
- coarse ground black pepper to taste
- optional ingredients: sliced black olives, capers, or diced pickle

Technique:

To prepare the "egg whites", place the "egg white" ingredients into a blender and process until smooth. Pour the mixture into a saucepan and bring to rapid simmer over medium heat, stirring frequently to avoid scorching the tofu mixture. Pour the mixture into any food storage container and set aside to cool.

Next, crumble the ⅔ pressed block of tofu into a food processor and add the mayo, nutritional yeast, prepared mustard, kala namak, turmeric and paprika. Process the contents until completely smooth, stopping as necessary to scrape down the sides of the food processor. Alternately, the mixture can be mashed using a fork but the mixture will not be as smooth.

Transfer the "yolk" mixture to a bowl or a food storage container and stir in the minced onion, celery, black pepper and any optional ingredients. Mix well, cover and refrigerate until ready to use. Cover the "egg white" container and refrigerate until the "egg whites" have completely set, or a minimum of 30 minutes.

Now, run a table knife around the perimeter of the "egg white" container to loosen if necessary and invert into a mixing bowl. Chop the "egg whites" with a table knife into fine dice or mash with a fork. Stir in the "yolk" mixture. Add additional mayonnaise as necessary to thoroughly moisten the eggless salad. Season the mixture with additional salt and pepper if desired, cover with plastic wrap and chill thoroughly before serving.

No-Eggy Mayo

This recipe produces an eggless mayonnaise that rivals real egg mayonnaise in both taste and texture and is much less expensive than commercial dairy/egg-free mayonnaise. The ingredients are readily available in most markets and an immersion blender or food processor makes this a nearly foolproof method for making mayonnaise.

The advantage of using a food processor is that the machine does most of the work for you. The advantage of using an immersion blender is that the mayonnaise will be thicker, yet requires less oil. The disadvantage of the immersion blender is that your hand and arm may become tired from controlling the blender.

The immersion blender method also requires a little dexterity to manage blending with one hand and pouring the oil with the other hand. If another person can help pour the oil, the process is much easier.

I have personally used both methods many, many times and now favor the immersion blender method for producing the best quality mayonnaise. It's definitely more of a chore, but the results are well worth it. A standard or high-powered blender is not recommended for making mayonnaise because once the mixture thickens, it's nearly impossible to keep it turning in the blades while adding the oil.

This is my own signature blend and yields about 2 cups of the finest egg-free mayonnaise.

Ingredients:

- ½ cup plain unsweetened soymilk with no additives, chilled (sorry, no substitutions)
- 1 T plus 1 tsp fresh lemon juice
- 1 tsp apple cider vinegar, preferably raw organic
- 2 tsp organic sugar
- 1 tsp dry ground mustard*
- 1 tsp sea salt or kosher salt
- pinch of ground white pepper
- pinch of paprika or cayenne pepper
- optional: pinch of kala namak (imparts an egg mayonnaise flavor)
- 1 and ½ cup mild vegetable oil if using an immersion blender; or 1 and ¾ cup mild vegetable oil if using a food processor

*Do not omit this ingredient! Dry ground mustard not only adds flavor but is a natural emulsifier and essential to the success of this recipe.

For garlic mayo, add 1 tsp minced garlic (1 clove) or ½ tsp garlic powder to the soymilk mixture. For wasabi mayo, add 1 tsp wasabi paste or ½ tsp wasabi powder to the soymilk mixture.

Technique:

Measure the oil into a liquid measuring cup (ideally it should have a "lip" for pouring). Set aside.

Immersion blender method:

Place all of the ingredients EXCEPT for the oil into a 4-cup glass measuring cup or heavy glass/ceramic bowl. Insert the immersion blender and process the mixture for about 10 seconds.

Now with the immersion blender running on high speed, SLOWLY drizzle the oil into the blending cup or bowl. Move the blender up and down and side to side as you add the oil. Continue blending until all the oil is incorporated and the mixture is emulsified and very thick. Transfer to a glass jar or plastic container and refrigerate.

Note: I cannot emphasize enough the importance of adding the oil slowly. If you add the oil too fast, the emulsion may break and revert back to a liquid.

Food processor method:

Place all of the ingredients EXCEPT for the oil into a food processor and process the mixture for about 10 seconds.

Turn the food processor on continuous run (if you have speed settings, run on high speed) and SLOWLY begin to drizzle the oil into the mixture through the food chute. The addition of the oil will take several minutes, so be patient and don't rush. You should begin to note a change in the consistency of the mixture after about 1 and ¼ cup of oil has been added. Continue to SLOWLY add the remainder of the oil. As soon as all of the oil has been incorporated, turn the processor off - the mayonnaise is finished. Transfer to a glass jar or plastic container and refrigerate.

Note: I cannot emphasize enough the importance of adding the oil slowly. If you add it too fast, the emulsion may break and revert back to a liquid.

Non-Dairy Treats

Classic Cheesecake

A rich and dense New York-style cheesecake made with cultured cream cheese.

Ingredients:

- 1 nine-inch Graham Cracker or Cookie Crumb Pie Shell (recipe follows)
- ½ block (6 oz.) extra-firm silken tofu
- 12 oz. (1 recipe) Cream Cheese (pg. 37)
- ¾ cup organic sugar
- ¾ cup water
- 2 T fresh lemon juice
- 3 T cornstarch or arrowroot powder
- 1 tsp real vanilla extract
- 1 tsp agar powder
- ¼ tsp sea salt

Technique:

Prepare and pre-bake the pie shell at 375°F for 12 minutes. Remove from the oven and set aside to cool. Leave the oven on.

Drain the silken tofu on several layers of paper towels for 20 minutes and then gently blot to remove as much moisture as possible.

Crumble the tofu into a blender and add the remaining ingredients. Process the contents until completely smooth, stopping to scrape down the sides of the blender as necessary with a rubber/silicone spatula.

Turn off the blender and stir the mixture with the spatula (this will help release any air bubbles in the mixture).

Pour the mixture into the pie crust. Smooth the top with the spatula to release any visible air bubbles. Place in a large, shallow baking dish that will accommodate the 9-inch pie plate.

Slowly pour HOT water into the shallow dish so that the bottom half of the pie plate is submerged (about ½-inch). Avoid overfilling and be careful not to splash water into the cheesecake mixture. The water bath will help the cheesecake to cook more evenly. Being careful not to tip the baking dish, place the dish in the oven and bake for 50 minutes.

Being careful not to tip the baking dish, remove the dish from the oven and set on a level surface to cool to near room temperature. Remove the cheesecake and place on a towel to dry the bottom of the pie plate. Cover with plastic wrap and refrigerate until completely chilled and firm.

Slice and serve with your favorite fresh fruit, fruit sauce or other toppings as desired.

Note: The surface of the cheesecake will feel dry to the touch and have a golden yellow hue after baking. The surface will return to a moist texture and light cream color after being covered with plastic wrap and refrigerated.

Graham Cracker or Cookie Crumb Pie Shell

Ingredients:

- 1 and ¾ cup dairy and egg free graham cracker or cookie crumbs
- 6 T melted Better Butter (pg. 12)

Technique:

Preheat the oven to 375°F. Mix all ingredients until well blended. Press firmly onto the bottom and up the sides of a 9-inch pie plate. Bake 12 minutes; cool completely, before filling.

Variations:

- ❖ For a nutty crust, reduce the graham crumbs to ¾ cup and add ½ cup finely chopped walnuts, pecans or almonds.
- ❖ For a spiced crust, add 1 tsp ground cinnamon and ½ tsp ground nutmeg.

Chocolate Mascarpone Cheesecake

A rich and dense New York-style chocolate cheesecake made with mascarpone cheese.

Ingredients:

- ½ carton (about 6 oz.) extra-firm silken tofu
- 1 nine-inch Graham Cracker or Cookie Crumb Pie Shell (pg. 136)
- 12 oz. (1 recipe) Mascarpone cheese (pg. 91)
- ¾ cup water
- 1 cup organic sugar
- ⅓ cup unsweetened cocoa powder
- 3 T cornstarch or arrowroot powder
- 2 tsp real vanilla extract
- 1 tsp agar powder
- ¼ tsp sea salt

Technique:

Drain the silken tofu on several layers of paper towels for 20 minutes and then gently blot to remove as much moisture as possible.

Prepare and pre-bake the pie crust in a 9-inch pie tin at 375°F for 12 minutes. Remove from the oven and set aside to cool. Leave the oven on.

Crumble the tofu into a blender and add remaining ingredients. Process the contents until completely smooth, stopping to scrape down the sides of the blender as necessary with a rubber/silicone spatula. Turn off the blender and stir the mixture with the spatula (this will help release any air bubbles in the mixture).

Pour the mixture into the pie crust. Smooth the top with the spatula to release any visible air bubbles. Place in a large, shallow baking dish that will accommodate the 9-inch pie plate.

Slowly pour HOT water into the shallow dish so that the bottom half of the pie plate is submerged (about ½-inch). Avoid overfilling and be careful not to splash water into the cheesecake mixture. The water bath will help the cheesecake to cook more evenly. Being careful not to tip the baking dish, place the dish in the oven and bake for 50 minutes.

Being careful not to tip the baking dish, remove the dish from the oven and set on a level surface to cool to near room temperature. Remove the cheesecake and place on a towel to dry the bottom of the pie plate. Cover with plastic wrap and refrigerate for several hours until completely chilled and firm. Slice and garnish with your favorite toppings as desired.

Note: The cheesecake will form its own chocolate "glaze" while baking.

Crème Caramel

Crème Caramel, or flan, is a custard dessert with a soft caramel glaze, as opposed to crème brûlée, which is a custard dessert with a hard caramel glaze. It's fairly easy to make and creates a beautiful dessert presentation. This recipe yields six ½-cup servings.

Ingredients for the custard:

- 1 carton (12.3 oz.) firm or extra-firm silken tofu, drained
- 1 can (13.5 oz.) organic unsweetened full-fat coconut milk
- ¾ cup organic sugar
- 2 tsp cornstarch or arrowroot powder
- 1 and ½ tsp agar powder
- 2 tsp real vanilla extract
- ¼ tsp ground cinnamon
- a pinch of freshly grated nutmeg

Ingredients for the caramel glaze:

- ½ cup light brown sugar
- 2 T water
- 2 T Better Butter (pg. 12)

Special items needed:

- any shallow, heat-proof, round or square bowl or pan that will hold a minimum of 3 cups liquid

Technique:

First, place all the custard ingredients in a blender and process until smooth. Pour into a medium saucepan and set aside.

To make the caramel, stir together the ½ cup light brown sugar and 2 tablespoons of water in a small saucepan until the sugar is dissolved. Add the butter or margarine and bring to a simmer. Reduce the heat to medium-low and continue to cook for exactly 4 minutes. Gently swirl the pan occasionally over the heat but do not stir. Keep warm over low heat until the custard is ready in the next step.

While the caramel mixture is cooking, bring the custard mixture to a simmer over medium heat, stirring frequently. Watch it carefully so it does not boil over. After the mixture has come to a simmer and thickened, remove the pan from the heat source.

Now carefully pour the caramel into the heat-proof custard mold. Tilt the mold in all directions to swirl the caramel evenly across the bottom and partially up the sides.

Now, immediately pour the custard mixture into the mold over the caramel. Let cool at room temperature for about 20 minutes. Cover with plastic wrap and refrigerate for several hours until set.

To remove the custard from the mold, carefully run a knife around the inside perimeter of the mold to loosen the custard. Fill the sink without about ½-inch of very hot water. Set the mold into the sink for few minutes. Wipe the bottom of the mold dry with a towel and place a serving plate on top. Quickly invert the custard onto the plate (you may have to shake the mold to release the custard). Slice and serve.

Horchata

Horchata is a sweetened Latin American rice beverage flavored with cinnamon and vanilla. It is served chilled over crushed ice.

Technique:

In the bottom of a 1 quart container, mix together 1 tsp ground cinnamon and 2 tsp real vanilla extract (the alcohol in the extract will dissolve the natural oil in the cinnamon which helps keep the cinnamon suspended in the Horchata). Pour in 1 quart of strained, warm Whole Rice Milk (pg. 16). Stir in an additional 2 tablespoons organic sugar and ¼ cup real maple syrup and mix thoroughly to dissolve the sugar. Chill and serve over crushed ice.

Fresh Fruit Ice Cream

Heavy non-dairy cream and puréed fruit form the base for this delightful frozen treat. An ice cream maker is required for this recipe.

Ingredients:

- 2 cups Heavy Cream (pg. 18)
- ¾ cup organic sugar
- ½ tsp guar gum
- 2 cups chilled fruit purée, smooth or semi-chunky

Technique:

Pour the heavy cream into a blender and add the sugar and guar gum; process until smooth. Pour the mixture into a container and refrigerate until very cold (or place in the freezer for about 30 minutes).

When well chilled, pour the cream mixture into your ice cream maker and add the chilled fruit purée. Process the mixture according to your ice cream maker's instructions.

Chocolate Cream Pie

A graham cracker or cookie crumb pie shell is filled with a silky chocolate filling and crowned with heavenly whipped cream. It's chocolaty, velvety and decadently delicious!

For the pie shell, you will need:

- 1 nine-inch Graham Cracker or Cookie Crumb Pie Shell (pg. 136)

Ingredients for the pie filling:

- 1 can (13.5 oz.) organic unsweetened full-fat coconut milk
- 1 carton (12.3 oz.) firm or extra-firm silken tofu
- ½ cup plain unsweetened non-dairy milk
- ¾ cup organic sugar
- ⅓ cup unsweetened cocoa powder
- ¼ cup (4 T) cornstarch or arrowroot powder
- ¼ tsp sea salt
- 2 tsp real vanilla extract

Topping:

- Heavenly Whipped Cream (pg. 21)

Technique:

Preheat the oven to 375°F. Bake the pie shell for 12 minutes. Remove and set aside to cool.

In a blender, process the coconut milk, silken tofu, non-dairy milk, sugar, cocoa powder, cornstarch or arrowroot powder, salt and vanilla until smooth. Transfer to a large saucepan and cook over medium heat, stirring frequently, until the mixture begins to bubble (the mixture will form lumps as you cook, this is normal; just keep stirring until the pudding becomes smooth).

Remove from the heat and pour into the pie crust. Smooth the top gently with a rubber/silicone spatula or the back of a spoon and place in the refrigerator uncovered for 1 hour until the top of the pie is set. Cover with plastic wrap and chill the pie for an additional 2 hours minimum, or until completely firm. Remove from the refrigerator and spread a layer of the whipped cream evenly over the pie before serving.

Lemon Meringue Pie

A graham cracker pie shell is filled with a tangy and refreshing lemon curd, crowned with optional meringue and lightly baked.

The meringue has a rather starchy flavor on its own, although the starchy flavor is less noticeable when paired with the lemon filling. As far as texture, it has more of a soft marshmallow consistency than a meringue consistency. It's worth trying however, and if you don't care for it you can always lift and remove the meringue from the pie after it has chilled. Another option is to top the pie with Heavenly Whipped Cream (pg. 21), or simply omit the topping altogether and garnish with fresh slices of lemon or candied lemon peel.

For the pie shell, you will need:

- 1 nine-inch Graham Cracker or Cookie Crumb Pie Shell (pg. 136)

Ingredients for the pie filling:

- 1 carton (12.3 oz.) firm or extra-firm silken tofu
- 1 and ¼ cup organic sugar
- 1 cup water
- ¾ cup fresh lemon juice
- 5 T cornstarch or arrowroot powder
- 1 T fresh grated lemon zest
- ¼ tsp sea salt

For the optional meringue:

- ½ cup organic sugar
- ½ cup water
- 6 T egg replacer powder (e.g., Ener-G™ egg replacer)

Technique:

Preheat the oven to 375°F. Bake the pie shell for 12 minutes. Remove and set aside to cool.

If you will be topping the pie with meringue, add ½ cup organic sugar to a DRY blender and process into a fine powder. Set aside in a small bowl.

Note: Do not use commercial powdered sugar for the meringue, vegan or otherwise, as it often contains significant amounts of starch which will upset the balance of starch in the egg replacer powder.

In the blender, process the pie filling ingredients until smooth. Pour the blender contents into a large saucepan and cook over medium heat, stirring frequently with a rubber or silicone spatula and scraping the sides of the saucepan as you stir. The mixture will be foamy and milky in appearance. Stir constantly as the mixture begins to thicken. Keep stirring until the mixture begins to bubble and the milky and foamy appearance transforms into a thick and gelatinous lemon curd.

Pour the filling into the pie crust, smooth the top gently with a rubber/silicone spatula or the back of a spoon and place in the refrigerator uncovered for 2 hours until the top of the pie is firmly set. If you are omitting the meringue, cover the pie with plastic wrap and chill several more hours until completely set. For the meringue, continue to the next step.

After the pie has chilled for 2 hours, preheat the oven to 210°F. In a large mixing bowl, add the egg replacer powder and ¼ cup of water. Beat with an electric mixer on high speed until peaks begin to form. Begin adding the finely powdered sugar and the remaining ¼ cup water in increments while continuing to beat on high speed. Beat for about 5 minutes until stiff peaks begin to form and the meringue is fluffy and voluminous.

Spoon and spread the meringue onto the surface of the pie, avoiding the edges by ½-inch. Bake in the oven for 30 minutes. Remove to cool at room temperature for about 5 minutes and then place in the refrigerator to chill thoroughly for several hours until completely set before serving. Keep refrigerated but do not cover or the meringue will turn into a gooey liquid.

Mini Lemon Meringue Tarts:

Prepare the pie filling according to the recipe. Fill individual frozen mini fillo cups with the filling and refrigerate as recommended. Then top with a small dollop of meringue and bake according to the directions. Refrigerate until chilled and serve.

Key Lime Pie

A graham cracker pie shell is filled with a citrusy and refreshing key lime curd. The pie can be topped with Heavenly Whipped Cream if desired, as the light coconut flavor pairs nicely with the tanginess of the lime; or simply garnish with additional lime wedges or zest.

For the pie shell, you will need:

- 1 nine-inch Graham Cracker or Cookie Crumb Pie Shell (pg. 136)

Ingredients for the pie filling:

- 1 carton (12.3 oz.) firm or extra-firm silken tofu
- 1 and ¼ cup organic sugar
- 1 cup water
- ¾ cup fresh key lime or regular lime juice
- 5 T cornstarch or arrowroot powder
- 1 T fresh grated key lime zest
- ¼ tsp sea salt

Technique:

Preheat the oven to 375°F. Bake the pie shell for 12 minutes. Remove and set aside to cool.

In a blender, process the pie filling ingredients until smooth. Pour the blender contents into a large saucepan and cook over medium heat, stirring frequently with a rubber or silicone spatula and scraping the sides of the saucepan as you stir. The mixture will be foamy and milky in appearance. Stir constantly as the mixture begins to thicken. Keep stirring until the mixture begins to bubble and the milky and foamy appearance transforms into a thick and gelatinous lime curd.

Pour the filling into the pie crust, smooth the top gently with a rubber/silicone spatula or the back of a spoon and place in the refrigerator uncovered for 2 hours until the top of the pie is firmly set. After 2 hours, cover with plastic wrap. Garnish with Heavenly Whipped Cream (pg. 21) and lime wedges or zest, if desired, before serving.

Banana Cream Pie

resh sliced bananas are layered in a graham cracker or cookie crumb pie shell, bathed in a creamy vanilla pudding and then crowned with Heavenly Whipped Cream.

Pie Ingredients:

- 1 nine-inch Graham Cracker or Cookie Crumb Pie Shell (pg. 136)
- 4 ripe large bananas
- Heavenly Whipped Cream (pg. 21)

Pie filling ingredients:

- ½ carton (6 oz.) extra-firm silken tofu, drained
- 1 and ¼ cup non-dairy milk
- 2 T plus 2 tsp cornstarch or arrowroot powder
- ½ cup organic sugar
- 2 tsp real vanilla extract
- pinch of sea salt
- pinch of fresh nutmeg (optional)

Technique:

Preheat the oven to 375°F. Bake the pie shell for 12 minutes. Remove and set aside to cool.

In a blender, process the pie filling ingredients until smooth. Pour the blender contents into a large saucepan and cook over medium heat, stirring frequently with a rubber or silicone spatula and scraping the sides of the saucepan as you stir. The mixture will be foamy and milky in appearance. Stir constantly as the mixture begins to thicken. Keep stirring until the mixture forms a thickened pudding. Remove from the heat.

Thinly slice the bananas and place a single layer on the bottom of the pie shell. Spoon about ⅓ of the pudding mixture over the bananas and spread evenly. Add another layer of bananas and half of the remaining mixture, again spreading evenly. Repeat with the last layer of bananas and finish with the remaining pudding mixture. Smooth the top gently with a rubber/silicone spatula.

Place in the refrigerator uncovered for 1 hour until the top of the pie is set. Cover with plastic wrap and chill the pie for several hours to completely set.

Remove from the refrigerator and spread a layer of the whipped cream or topping evenly over the pie. Garnish with sliced bananas or chocolate curls just before serving, if desired. Store in the refrigerator gently covered in plastic wrap and consume within a couple of days before the bananas turn brown.

Coconut Cream Pie

A graham cracker pie shell is filled with a velvety coconut cream, and then crowned with vega̶
whipped topping and toasted coconut. Everyone deserves to indulge now and then, especially
when this pie is so easy to make. This is one of my favorite desserts.

For the pie shell you will need:

- 1 nine-inch Graham Cracker or Cookie Crumb Pie Shell (pg. 136)

Ingredients for the filling:

- 1 cup coconut flakes, sweetened or unsweetened - your choice
- 1 can (13.5 oz.) organic unsweetened full-fat coconut milk
- 1 carton (about 12 oz.) firm/extra-firm silken tofu
- ⅔ cup organic sugar
- ½ cup plain unsweetened non-dairy milk
- ¼ cup (4 T) cornstarch (preferably non-GMO) or arrowroot powder
- ¼ tsp sea salt
- 1 tsp real vanilla extract
- Heavenly Whipped Cream (pg. 21)

Technique:

Spread the coconut flakes on a cookie sheet and bake in the oven at 375°F for about 5 minutes, or until the coconut turns a light golden brown just around the edges. Set aside to cool. Pre-bake your pie crust at the same time, but bake for about 12 minutes or until lightly browned.

In a blender, process the coconut milk, silken tofu, non-dairy milk, sugar, cornstarch or arrowroot powder, salt and vanilla until smooth.

Pour the blender contents into a large saucepan and cook over medium heat, stirring constantly with a rubber or silicone spatula and scraping the sides of the saucepan as you stir. Cook until the mixture becomes very thick and starts to bubble (the mixture will form lumps as you cook, this is normal; just keep stirring until the pudding becomes smooth).

Remove from the heat and add ¾ cup of the toasted coconut (reserving ¼ cup for the topping on the pie). Stir well. Pour into the pie crust, smooth the top gently with a rubber/silicone spatula or the back of a spoon and place in the refrigerator uncovered for 1 hour until the top of the pie is set. Cover with plastic wrap and chill the pie for an additional 2 hours minimum, or until completely firm.

Remove from the refrigerator and spread a layer of the whipped cream or topping evenly over the pie. Sprinkle with the remaining ¼ cup toasted coconut.

Milk Chocolate Pudding

Rich, creamy and delicious, the texture of this pudding is reminiscent of a mousse. This recipe yields about 3 cups or six ½ cup servings. A fine mesh strainer is required for this recipe.

Ingredients:

- ½ cup (2.5 oz. by weight) whole raw cashews
- 2 and ½ cups non-dairy milk
- 2 T cornstarch or arrowroot powder
- ¾ cup organic sugar
- ⅓ cup unsweetened cocoa powder
- 1 T real vanilla extract
- ¼ tsp sea salt or kosher salt

Technique:

Place the cashews and non-dairy milk in a container with a lid, cover and soak for a minimum of 8 hours in the refrigerator.

Place the strainer over a large glass bowl or BPA-free plastic storage container and set aside. Add the milk, cashews and the remaining ingredients to a blender and process on high speed for 2 full minutes. Stop to scrape down the sides of the blender as necessary.

Pour the mixture into a large saucepan and place over medium heat. Stir slowly and continually with a whisk. Whisk vigorously as the mixture begins to thicken (vigorous whisking will help to prevent lumps from forming). Continue whisking until the mixture begins to bubble.

Pour the mixture into the strainer and stir with the whisk to press the mixture through the mesh. Cover the container with plastic wrap and let cool for about 15 minutes and then refrigerate for several hours until well-chilled.

To serve, stir the mixture thoroughly and spoon into individual dessert cups. Garnish the individual cups with Heavenly Whipped Cream (pg. 21), if desired.

Spiced Vanilla Pudding

Rich, creamy and lightly spiced with cinnamon and nutmeg, the texture of this vanilla pudding is reminiscent of a mousse and can be served as a dessert on its own or used as a pastry filling. This recipe yields about 3 cups or six ½ cup servings. A fine mesh strainer is required for this recipe.

Ingredients:

- ½ cup (2.5 oz. by weight) whole raw cashews
- 2 and ½ cups non-dairy milk
- 2 T cornstarch or arrowroot powder
- ¾ cup organic sugar
- 1 T real vanilla extract or the "caviar" scraped from 1 split vanilla bean
- ¼ tsp sea salt
- ¼ tsp ground cinnamon
- ⅛ tsp (a pinch) fresh grated nutmeg

Technique:

Place the cashews and non-dairy milk in a container with a lid, cover and soak for a minimum of 8 hours in the refrigerator.

Place the strainer over a large glass bowl or BPA-free plastic storage container and set aside. Add the milk, cashews and the remaining ingredients to a blender and process on high speed for 2 full minutes. Stop to scrape down the sides of the blender as necessary.

Pour the mixture into a large saucepan and place over medium heat. Stir slowly and continually with a whisk. Whisk vigorously as the mixture begins to thicken (vigorous whisking will help to prevent lumps from forming). Continue whisking until the mixture begins to bubble.

Pour the mixture into the strainer and stir with the whisk to press the mixture through the mesh. Cover the container with plastic wrap and let cool for about 15 minutes and then refrigerate for several hours until well-chilled.

To serve, stir the mixture thoroughly and spoon into individual dessert cups. Garnish the individual cups with Heavenly Whipped Cream (pg. 21) and an additional pinch of fresh grated nutmeg before serving, if desired.

Holiday Pumpkin 'Nog

A rich and creamy non-dairy and egg-free concoction blended with pumpkin purée and flavored with cinnamon, nutmeg, ginger and clove. Spike with your favorite liquor, if desired, such as brandy or rum and garnish with a dollop of Heavenly Whipped Cream and a dash of freshly grated nutmeg. Pumpkin 'nog is also fantastic when added to hot coffee! This recipe yields about 5 cups.

Ingredients:

- 7.5 oz. (½ of a 15 oz. can) pumpkin purée
- 1 carton (1 qt./4 cups) non-dairy milk of your choice
- ⅔ cup organic sugar
- 1 T nutritional yeast
- 2 tsp real vanilla extract
- 1 tsp ground cinnamon
- ½ tsp ground ginger
- ¼ tsp freshly grated nutmeg plus additional for garnish
- ¼ tsp ground cloves
- pinch of sea salt
- optional: liquor of your choice
- optional garnish: Heavenly Whipped Cream (pg. 21)

Technique:

Process all the ingredients (except for the optional liquor and optional whipped cream) in a blender until completely smooth, about 1 minute. Chill thoroughly. Stir or shake before serving and stir in the optional liquor. Pour into individual glasses and garnish with the optional whipped cream and grated nutmeg. Store refrigerated and consume within 10 days.

Made in the USA
Lexington, KY
21 October 2013